HOME BAKED

A little book of bread, cake
and biscuit recipes

George & Cecilia Scurfield

GRUB STREET · LONDON

Published in 2009 by
Grub Street
4 Rainham Close
London
SW11 6SS
Email: food@grubstreet.co.uk
Web: www.grubstreet.co.uk

First published by Faber and Faber as *Home Baked* in 1956 and
Home-Made Cakes and Biscuits in 1963

A CIP record for this title is available from the British Library
ISBN 978-1-906502-37-9

Printed and bound by MPG, Bodmin, Cornwall on FSC (Forest
Stewardship Council) paper

Publisher's note
These two books, now combined into one volume, were first
published almost 50 years ago. Apart from adding metric measures
to aid contemporary readers, the text remains unaltered to retain
the integrity and charm of what have become regarded as classic
works much admired by Elizabeth David.

CONTENTS

INTRODUCTION

A few years ago we got fed up with shop bread. Even when quite fresh, it was unappetising; it was often poor in texture; sometimes it fell to bits on the board when we tried to slice it. And very often it wouldn't keep at all. As for wholemeal bread, this was practically unobtainable; the brown loaves we were offered seemed like very distant cousins, several times removed.

We decided to bake our own bread. We had done this before occasionally but now we would go in for it more seriously. We were lucky enough to be living near a mill which still proudly produced a delightfully nutty, stone-ground, wholemeal flour. Their white flour, too, really tasted of wheat and was not just a fine, white powder like the tasteless stuff you buy in packets from the grocer.

The quality of our bread—its taste, texture and the way it kept—surprised us. And friends who tasted it became very excited about it, especially the stone-ground, wholemeal bread. You couldn't buy anything like it in the shops, they said. And it suddenly occurred to us that here perhaps was a means of making money.

We started a little bakery in our kitchen.

It's no easy matter, in these days of Town and Country Planning and Sanitary Inspection and rules and regulations, to start anything, but if the authorities were not exactly enthusiastic about us our customers certainly were. We started with a dozen and within two or three months we had over a hundred. There was a limit to what we could bake and deliver, however, and eventually we found that we should either have to go in for the business properly and operate on a different, impersonal basis, or we should have to devote all our lives, every minute of them, to the baking, and this we did not want to do.

We closed down. But not before we had explored the pleasures of yeast cookery, not before we had tried out and experimented with all sorts of yeast recipes and discovered that the liberal use of yeast in the kitchen opens up a prospect of boundless delights.

At the same time we discovered that a good many people are frightened of baking their own bread. Perhaps they are put off by the idea of all the kneading, or they're mystified by the way yeast works, or they don't think they've got the right sort of oven, or they imagine they will have to go round draught-proofing their kitchen and all that sort of nonsense; whatever the reason, it is apparently a fact that most housewives, in the south of England anyway, do not like the idea of baking their own bread at home.

They don't know what they're missing.

And now that it's no longer a trade secret, so to speak, we would like to explain just how simple and foolproof bread making is.

In the first chapter we're going to concentrate on plain, ordinary bread and how it can be made in the most trouble-free way, with the most delicious results.

Once you have made and tasted your own bread it's most unlikely that you will want to return, permanently, to shop bread.

Once you have made a plain bread dough and learned the feel of it, once you have seen it rise and shaped it into loaves, and once you have watched them prove and baked them to your satisfaction, then the whole field of yeast cookery lies waiting for you. While we were baking we tried to introduce a new 'fancy line' every week or so—French bread, Coffee bread, Croissants, Brioches and so on. Everyone knows how delightful these things are to eat but not everyone is aware how easy they are to prepare.

On the whole baking with yeast is easier and more foolproof than making cakes. Yeast is certainly less agitating to work with than baking powder.

And so when we've covered the simple bread recipes we would like to deal with some of the more exciting things that can be made with yeast. We thought it might be useful to have a representative selection of bread and yeast recipes collected together between the covers of one little book.

We have divided these 'fancy' recipes roughly into two sorts—English Tea Breads and Coffee Breads from Abroad. We have included another miscellaneous section for those recipes that don't seem to fit into either category.

The great thing about baking with yeast is the difficulty of failure.

If you find the dough doesn't rise, wait just a little longer; it surely will rise if you haven't forgotten the yeast altogether, and even if you have left it out you can always add it with a little more liquid and flour and set the dough to rise once more. Again, there's no need to worry if you get some of the ingredients weighed out incorrectly. Flour varies in absorbency anyway, and eggs vary in size and fat in oiliness, and so on. You can always add more flour if the dough is too slack, or more liquid if it's too dry.

Really the only thing that can go wrong when baking is leaving the loaves in the oven and forgetting all about them until they've become nothing more than charred remains.

Before we go any further we would like to say something about flour, and yeast.

Most people who make their own bread begin doing so because they are not satisfied with their baker's wholemeal bread. This may be because he is a bad baker, because of modern steam bakeries, forced rising and the rest, or because of the poor quality of his flour; it may be that his wholemeal bread is not really made from wholemeal flour at all but from a blended and artificial mixture.

Until the introduction of the roller mill in the second half of the nineteenth century, all flour was stone-ground. That is to say, the wheat was cleaned, and then ground between stones in one operation. (If you wanted white flour it had to be sieved, or bolted. The white flour of the rich, a hundred and fifty years ago, cannot have been very white.)

The roller mill is really a whole series of mills and it doesn't harm the wheat in any way but it enables the miller to separate the flour, the bran, the middlings and the germ. These can of course be blended together again in any proportions you like though normally the bran and the middlings go for stock-feed while the germ is used in many proprietary vitamin preparations.

The white flour from a roller mill, whatever the extraction rate—if the extraction rate is, say, 72, that means 72 parts of flour from 100 parts whole wheat, so the higher the better from a nutritional point of view—and although it may have been enriched with calcium and vitamins, can hardly be of the same food value as plain, wholemeal flour nothing added, nothing taken away.

But most people, children especially, prefer white bread, and if, in other ways, they eat normal, healthy foods, with a fair amount of green vegetables, meat and milk, they should get a plentiful supply of all the vitamins, proteins and minerals they require. (If you do happen to have a small child who only likes to eat white bread, and hardly any other food at all, then why not give him white bread that's been enriched in the making with milk and eggs and fat?)

All the same, white bread cannot truly qualify as the staff of life. And the taste, not to mention the texture and the keeping qualities, of home-made bread made from stone-ground, wholemeal wheat flour is so much pleasanter, so much nuttier that it really seems unnecessary to go into all the nutritional reasons there may be for preferring it.

We find, moreover that there is little or no wastage with home-made bread, brown or white, whereas with shop bread we were continually throwing crusts and ends of loaves into the swill bucket.

Unfortunately it is sometimes difficult to obtain supplies of wholemeal flour. You cannot blame the millers for their tendency to give up stone grinding; the public gets what it asks for, and since 1914 something like 96 per cent of all the bread eaten in England has been white.

But there are still quite a few mills that do stone grind wholemeal wheat flour. And you can always buy it at your nearest health food stores, or similar shop. Bought in small 3 lb bags at a grocer's, however, it will work out very expensive; your bread will cost you considerably more than baker's bread. (For a small baker the profit margin on a loaf of bread, subsidy included, is almost non-existent; he makes his living, if he makes one at all, out of his 'fancies'.) And if you're going to bake any quantity of bread at all—and this applies to all flours—it will be much cheaper to buy it in large quantities, by the ½ or ¼ sack, 10 or 5 stone, direct from a mill.

Try your local millers and you may have a pleasant surprise and find one that still produces stone-ground flour.

Not only will your flour be cheaper like this, it will probably also be fresher and make better bread and cakes. A grocer has to know about a great many things, he is unlikely to be a flour specialist. But that is exactly what a miller is. Flour is his life, and he can and will advise you and supply you with whatever kind of flour you require—for bread, for cakes, for biscuits or for pastry. (Most millers will let you have as little as a stone at a time.) And if you want something rather exotic, like rye flour, that he can't supply, he will surely put you in touch with a miller who can.

If kept in any dry, mouse-proof container (a small dustbin will take 5 stone nicely), the flour, even wholemeal which doesn't keep as well as white, will stay in perfect condition for 3 or 4 months and longer.

As for yeast—there should be no difficulty in obtaining supplies of fresh, compressed baker's yeast, which is the easiest to work with. Any baker, if he is a baker and not just a retailer of factory-made bread, will let you have some. And your local health food stores should certainly be able to supply you.

If you can't get fresh, compressed, baker's yeast, the dried yeast that most big grocers stock is perfectly satisfactory for ordinary bread. This should be used in half the quantities recommended for fresh yeast. Dried yeast has rather a strong, beery flavour, though, and cannot be recommended for those 'fancy' recipes which demand a high proportion of yeast to flour. Dried yeast takes a little time to dissolve in warm water and is perhaps not so easy to cream as fresh yeast. Fresh yeast, by the way, will remain in good condition for 10 days or a fortnight if stored in a refrigerator, some distance from the freezing unit—it should be kept wrapped in greaseproof paper or in a covered bowl.

ACKNOWLEDGEMENTS

When we were running our bakery we browsed our way through a great many cookery books. We should like to mention the following in particular (to the authors of which, alive and dead, our thanks are due, as they started us off on many of our 'lines'):

Mrs. Beeton's Family Cookery. Ward Lock (no date).

Tante Marie's French Kitchen, translated and adapted by Charlotte Turgeon. Nicholas Kaye, 1950.

The Cereals Section of the Concise Encyclopedia of Gastronomy by Andre L. Simon. Collins, 1952.

The Viennese Cookery Book by Irma Rhode. Lehmann, 1952.

German Cooking by Robin Howe. André Deutsch, 1953.

Italian Cooking by Robin Howe. André Deutsch, 1953.

Jewish Cookery by Leah W. Leonard. André Deutsch, 1951.

Swedish Food, ed. Widdenfeld. Published by Effeltelf, Goteborginduftrir, Sweden, 1948.

We also have to thank *House & Garden* for permission to use material that first appeared in the pages of that magazine.

And we are very grateful, too, to James Nutter (Fulbourn) Ltd. who were so kind as to show us round their mill and who told us everything we know about flour and milling.

WEIGHTS AND MEASURES

All our recipes are given in pounds and ounces, and grams and pints, milliliters etc, and our tablespoons are English tablespoons.

But, if anyone wants to go exploring in cookery books it may be useful to know that:

1 cup flour is 4oz/110g

1 cup butter is 8oz/225g

1 cup milk is 8 fluid oz/250ml

A cup equals half an American pint which is 16 fluid oz (English pint is 20).

Two American tablespoons equal one English.

OVEN TEMPERATURES

	°F	°C	Gas
Very hot	450 – 475	230 – 240	8 – 9
Hot	400 – 450	200 – 240	6 – 8
Fairly hot	375 – 400	190 – 200	5 – 6
Moderate	350 – 375	180 – 190	4 – 5
Warm	325 – 350	160 – 180	3 – 4
Cool	275 – 325	140 – 160	1 – 3
Very cool	225 – 375	110 – 140	¼ – 1

The instruction manual with your gas cooker will tell you the appropriate settings of the thermostat. On most cookers 7 is about 410° F. (the right temperature to start baking loaves of bread). And to reach this heat most gas ovens will need to be pre-heated for about 15 minutes.

To reach the same heat an electric oven will require 30 minutes' pre-heating.

If you're using a solid-fuel cooker and you're uncertain about the oven temperatures you will find all you need to know in the Instruction Manual. But normally, it's best to start baking in the hottest oven.

WHOLEMEAL BREAD AND ROLLS
THE SIMPLE BREAD RECIPE AND OTHER PLAIN BREAD AND ROLLS

WHOLEMEAL BREAD – THE SIMPLE BREAD RECIPE
To make four small loaves.

INGREDIENTS
2½ lb/1.1kg stone-ground wholemeal flour
1oz/25g fresh yeast, or ½ oz/15g dried yeast
2oz/50g fat (butter, margarine or lard)
½ oz/15g salt
2 pints/1.2 litres warm water—the amount of water required will
vary according to the absorbency of the flour

METHOD
Put the flour in a large bowl. Make a well in the middle. Sprinkle the
salt round the edge. Cream the yeast with a little of the water and
pour it into the well. Add the fat, warmed and liquid, but not too
hot. Pour in the water, but not all at once, sometimes you need more,

sometimes less. And mix all the ingredients, lightly and thoroughly, with the fingers; this will make kneading easier.

KNEADING

Work through the dough with your fingers and thumbs. Pummel it and punch it and turn it over and over. If you find it easier take the dough out of the bowl and knead it on a board. Go on kneading for about 15 or 20 minutes. What you must aim at is a pleasant, smooth, springy dough of a putty-like consistency. The consistency changes quite suddenly when the dough is ready.

RISING

When the dough is kneaded to your satisfaction, cover the bowl with a damp cloth, and a lid to stop the cloth from drying out, and put it in a warm place to rise. The dough should rise for about 2 hours or until it has doubled in size. In wintertime the linen cupboard is a good place to put it, but in summer the warmth of a draughty kitchen is quite sufficient. The simplest thing, however, is to let the dough rise overnight—in the warmth of your kitchen or living room or even wrapped in an old eiderdown or blanket—and then use it as you want it during the following day.

SHAPING

When the dough has risen take it from the bowl and cut it into four and shape into loaves and put them on a lightly floured baking sheet to prove. Or put the dough into well-greased bread tins. (The dough for tins should be a little slacker (wetter) than that for shaped loaves.) Half fill the tins with dough, pressed well down—you don't want ugly folds in your bread.

PROVING

You can use the linen cupboard again for the proving. Or you can stand the loaves near a small fire. Or, if you've got a solid fuel cooker or boiler just place them on top of that—on the warm part, not the hot, they don't want too much heat, moderate warmth is all that's required. Don't worry about draughts. It's heat rather than cold that kills the yeast. A croissant dough will double its size overnight in a refrigerator. And if the dough hasn't been coddled, made to rise too quickly, everything will be all right.

(The man who brought our meat, when we were baking, had been trained as a master baker, and he was scornful of our efforts. 'Draughts will kill anything,' he used to say, looking round at our open doors and windows. But in fact, the draughts never killed anything.)

The loaves should prove for 45 minutes or an hour. You can easily tell when they are ready for the oven: they will be soft and slightly puffy to touch. On the whole it's better to underprove rather than overprove; loaves that have proved too long will be very bad in texture.

BAKING

For the first half hour the bread wants to go into a hot oven. Then turn the loaves round and let them stay in a moderate or fairly hot oven for another 20 minutes or half an hour. (You should try for conditions resembling the old baker's oven, where the fire was lit inside the oven itself and then raked out when full heat had been raised.)

Of course these oven heats can be varied somewhat according to how you like your bread baked, but 45 minutes is a minimum baking time.

When you finally remove the loaves from the oven put them on a wire tray to cool.

WHOLEMEAL ROLLS

To make about 3 dozen bread rolls.

INGREDIENTS

the same as for wholemeal bread

METHOD

The same as for the wholemeal bread until you come to the shaping. Then all you have to do is to shape the little rolls between the fingers and put them on a lightly floured baking sheet to prove. They need 20 minutes or half an hour to prove and about 15 minutes to bake in a hot oven—it's just as well to turn them round half way through.

These rolls will prove quite nicely on top of a gas oven while it's being pre-heated.

QUICK WHOLEMEAL BREAD

If you are in a hurry or you suddenly run out of bread you can bake a quick loaf simply by mixing and kneading a rather wet dough (otherwise just the same as for ordinary Wholemeal Bread) and putting it straight into tins and letting it prove for 45 minutes and then putting it in the oven. This bread will be perfectly satisfactory, though it won't be so light as the ordinary bread and it won't keep so well.

(The real advantage of the double rise, the ordinary method, is that you can make as much dough as you like at any one moment and bake when it's convenient. If you're not ready for it, or you can't get it all into the oven in one lot, you can just leave it. The yeast will go on working for a long time.

And it's very pleasant to have fresh rolls for breakfast on Sunday and this is very simple and scarcely any trouble if you make the dough some time on Saturday afternoon or evening.)

WHITE BREAD
To make 4 small loaves.

INGREDIENTS
2½ lb/1.1kg white flour
1oz/25g fresh yeast, or ½ oz/15g dried
2oz/50g fat (butter, margarine or lard)
½ oz/15g salt
About 1½ pints/900ml warm water

METHOD
The simple bread recipe, as for WHOLEMEAL BREAD. WHITE
ROLLS and QUICK WHITE BREAD can be made in exactly the
same way as the wholemeal, only substituting white flour for
wholemeal and using rather less water.

HALF-AND-HALF BREAD
Makes a pleasant change. To make 4 small loaves.

INGREDIENTS
1½ lb/700g white flour
1 lb/450g wholemeal flour
1oz/25g fresh yeast or ½ oz/15g dried
2oz/50g fat
½ oz/15g salt
1½ pints/900ml warm water (approx.)

METHOD
The simple bread recipe, as for WHOLEMEAL BREAD.

VIENNA BREAD
To make 4 small loaves.

INGREDIENTS
2½ lb/1.1kg white flour
1oz/25g fresh yeast, or ½ oz/15g dried
4oz/110g butter or margarine
½ oz/15g salt
1 pint/600ml warm milk, plus warm water as required

METHOD
The simple bread recipe, as for WHOLEMEAL BREAD. Special attention can be paid to the shaping of the loaves and the crusts should be painted with rich milk when the loaves are turned round.

BRIDGE ROLLS
To make about 3 dozen bridge rolls.

INGREDIENTS
2½ lb/1.1kg white flour
1oz/25g fresh yeast or ½ oz/15g dried
4 oz/110g butter or margarine
½ oz/15g salt
2 eggs
1 pint/600ml warm milk, plus water if required

METHOD
The simple bread recipe, as for WHOLEMEAL ROLLS. The eggs should be whisked up with the milk before adding to the flour. The rolls should be shaped into little sausages and painted with milk immediately before baking.

RYE BREAD

There are many different types of Rye bread. Nearly every Continental country has its own varieties. The nutritive value of rye is almost as great as wheat, and indeed rye flour contains some valuable food elements that wheat lacks.

If you want Rye flour ask your local miller if he knows who can supply you. It is normally milled in three grades, ranging from a fine, light rye flour to wholemeal.

LIGHT RYE BREAD

Using the simple bread recipe (as for WHOLEMEAL BREAD) and a 50–50 mixture of light Rye flour and ordinary white wheat flour you can produce a pleasant enough Rye loaf. But apart from a slight stickiness in texture there will be little to distinguish this from ordinary bread.

To obtain the essential Rye flavour you must use a sour dough.

SOUR DOUGH PASTE

A few days before you want to make your bread mix two or three tablespoonfuls of Rye flour with a little warm milk and make a paste. Leave this covered in a bowl in the warmth of your kitchen until it smells pleasantly sour.

Then you are ready to make your Rye bread. The following method is most satisfactory. The flour proportions can of course be varied according to individual taste. (You can use only Rye flour.)

SOUR RYE BREAD
To make 4 small loaves.

INGREDIENTS
1½ lb/700g wholemeal rye flour
1 lb/450g plain white flour (wheat)
½ oz/15g salt
4oz/110g fat
1 pint/600ml warm milk, and warm water as required (sour milk is better)
½ oz/15g fresh yeast or ¼ oz/6g dried
And the Sour Dough Paste

Strictly speaking the yeast is unnecessary. The Sour Dough Paste should be perfectly satisfactory as a leavening agent, but the yeast saves anxiety.

METHOD
Put all the flour and the salt in a large bowl and mix well together. Make a well and pour in the Sour Dough Paste and the fat, warmed and liquid but not too hot. Add the yeast, creamed in a little of the milk.

And then the kneading, the rising and the proving are the same as for the simple bread recipe (WHOLEMEAL BREAD) except that it is perhaps easier to make tin loaves. (As far as rising and proving is concerned Rye is a little tricky, and in our experience rye flour varies more from sack to sack than wheat.)

BAKING
This Rye bread should go into a fairly hot oven for half an hour. Then, when turning it round, paint the crust with milk or salt water, and bake in a moderate to cool oven for at least another hour and a half.

If you put a small ball of the dough in a bowl, cover it with milk and put it on one side, you will have a Sour Dough Paste all ready for the next baking. This paste will keep for about a fortnight.

QUICK RYE BREAD

The Sour Rye makes as satisfactory a quick bread as any we have tried. And the dough requires very little kneading—5 minutes are often enough, or until you've got a nice, smooth dough. Unfortunately it does take rather a long time to prove and bake, and you can't hurry Rye bread—if it's baked too soon or too fast then it tends to crack and split and is not very satisfactory.

FRENCH BREADS

To make 4 small loaves (or flutes).

STAGE 1. INGREDIENTS
1 lb/450g white flour
1oz/25g fresh yeast
½ pint/300ml warm water

METHOD

Put the flour in a bowl. Make a well. Cream the yeast very carefully and thoroughly with some of the water and pour it into the well. Add the rest of the water. Mix and knead until all the water has been absorbed. Then cover the bowl with a dry cloth and put it in a warm place to rise for about 3 hours—or overnight.

STAGE 2. INGREDIENTS
1 lb/450g flour
½ oz/15g salt
½ pint/300ml warm water
And the dough you've already made

METHOD

Dissolve the salt in the water and pour it all over the dough, which will have a crusty skin on it. Mix up well until you have got rid of the skin. Then gradually add the flour and knead for as long as you like. The longer the better, for the object is to make the dough as light as possible, but 10 or 15 minutes will be sufficient. Then lift the dough and slap it down into the bowl, again and again; go on doing this for a few minutes, as long as you can stand it! Cover the bowl with a damp cloth and put it back in a warm place to rise for at least 2 hours.

STAGE 3. METHOD

Divide the dough into 4 equal portions. Roll each piece into a ball and leave for 15 minutes covered with a dry cloth, on a floured board.

Now spread a clean tea cloth on a baking sheet and sprinkle it liberally with flour.

When the 15 minutes are up shape each ball into a long strand sausage by rolling and pulling, as long and as thin a strand as your baking sheet will take comfortably. Then lay the loaves you have thus fashioned on the cloth, pulling the cloth well up between the loaves and at each side, to prevent the bread from expanding outwards. Cover the whole with another cloth and allow to prove in moderate warmth for 1 hour.

Then roll the loaves very gently off the cloth, one by one, on to the baking sheet. Touch them as little as possible—they shouldn't have stuck to the cloth if it was well floured, but if they have a wooden spoon is better than fingers for removing them.

Make two or three shallow cuts on each loaf with a very sharp knife (a razor-blade knife is best) and bake in a hot oven for about 1 hour. The oven door should not be opened for the first half hour, and then they'll probably need turning and the crusts can be painted with melted butter or margarine or milk.

SODA BREAD
To make 2 medium-sized loaves.

INGREDIENTS
2 lb/900g flour (white or wholemeal)
½ oz/15g salt
2 teaspoons bicarbonate of soda and 2 of cream of tartar—or
1oz/25g baking powder
2oz/50g melted butter or margarine
1 pint/600ml milk, preferably sour or buttermilk

METHOD
Put the flour and the salt and the raising agents in a bowl and mix very thoroughly. Make a well and pour in the milk and the melted fat. Mix quickly, lightly and carefully. Divide the dough into two and shape into loaves and place on a floured baking sheet. Brush over with milk and bake in a hot oven for about 45 minutes.

GILDING THE LOAF

One of the secrets of making supremely edible-looking and appetizing bread is the shape and finish of the loaves and rolls.

You shape the loaves before you put them out to prove.

TO MAKE A COTTAGE LOAF
Roll one large ball of dough and put it on the baking sheet. Roll a smaller ball (about a third the size of the first) and place that on top of the first and press a floury finger right down through the middle of both.

TO MAKE A PLAIT
Divide the dough into 3, 5 or 7 equal portions. Roll each of these between fingers and hands until they are long thin strands, then plait them together just as if you were plaiting a rope or a girl's hair. It's generally best to plait loosely rather than tightly.

TO MAKE A BUN TWIST

Simply roll out the dough into a long sausage and tie the ends loosely together—as if tying a knot.

TO MAKE A VIENNESE TWIST

Roll out the dough into a tapering strand, about 2 feet long, as thick as your fist one end, and as thin as you like at the other. Then roll it up into a coil, starting from the thick end so that the thinner portions form graduated steps. Finally twist the tail over the top and smooth the whole thing into a nice oval.

FOR BUNS AND MUFFINS, ETC.

It's much easier to roll out the dough flat on a floured board and cut them out with a sharp knife or a tumbler than to pull handfuls of dough out of the bowl and shape between the fingers.

THE FINISH

If you want your plain loaves to have a gleaming, brown crust paint them with rich milk or cream before putting them in the oven (or when you turn them round). Painted with beaten egg they will have a darker crust, almost black. If you want them to have a crisp, crunchy crust, paint them with melted butter or margarine.

And if you want your sweet loaves and buns to shine in a most beautiful and sticky way, paint them with a thick milk and sugar syrup as soon as they come out of the oven. The difference this makes to the look of a fruit loaf is quite extraordinary.

ENGLISH TEA BREADS

CURRANT BREAD (FRUIT LOAF)
To make 2 medium-sized loaves.

INGREDIENTS
1½ lb/700g white flour
1oz/25g fresh yeast
4oz/110g butter or margarine
4oz/110g sugar
Pinch of salt
½ pint/300ml warm milk
4oz/110g sultanas
4oz/110g currants
2oz/50g candied peel

METHOD
Put the flour in a large bowl. Mix in the sugar and the salt. Make a well. Pour in the yeast, creamed in a little of the milk. Add the butter,

warmed and liquid but not too hot, and the rest of the milk. Knead thoroughly, adding warm water if required, and cover with a damp cloth and put in a warm place to rise for 1½ hours or until the dough has doubled in size. Then knock the dough down and knead in the fruit and shape into loaves (or use tins, half filled with the dough, pressed well down). Prove for 45 minutes and bake for 30 to 45 minutes in a moderate to fairly hot oven, turning the loaves round after the first 20 minutes. Paint the loaves with a thick milk and sugar syrup as soon as you have taken them from the oven.

This same dough makes excellent CURRANT BUNS. And many kinds of fruit bread can be made by varying the fruit (try dates and raisins, for example) and the flour. A SULTANA LOAF, made entirely with wholemeal flour, makes very pleasant eating.

MALT BREAD
To make 2 medium-sized loaves.

INGREDIENTS
1 lb/450g stone-ground wholemeal flour
4oz/110g white flour
Pinch of salt
1oz/25g fresh yeast
About ¾ pint/450ml warm water
2oz/50g butter or margarine
2 tablespoons black treacle
2 tablespoons extract of malt
2oz/50g sultanas (if you like)

METHOD
Put the flour and the salt in a large bowl and mix. Make a well. Pour in the yeast, creamed in a little of the water. Add the treacle, the malt extract, the butter, warmed and liquid but not too hot, and the water (as required). Knead until the dough is of even texture and all the malt and treacle have been blended in. Cover with a damp cloth and

leave to rise in a warm place for 2 hours or until the dough has doubled in size. Put the dough into tins, pressed well down, and prove for 45 minutes. Bake in a moderate oven for 45 minutes, turning the loaves round after the first 25 minutes. Paint the loaves with a thick milk and sugar syrup as soon as you have taken them from the oven and removed them from their tins.

Malt Bread keeps very well, even improves after 2 or 3 days. And this mixture makes very good MALT BUNS, too.

OATMEAL BREAD
To make 2 small loaves.

INGREDIENTS
8oz/225g medium oatmeal
¾ pint/450ml milk
½ oz/15g fresh yeast
2oz/50g butter or margarine
4 teaspoons salt
And about 8oz/225g flour (white or wholemeal)

METHOD
Put the oatmeal in a large bowl. Pour on the milk and leave to soak for at least 2 hours.

Then add the yeast, creamed in a very little warm water, the fat, warmed and liquid but not too hot, the salt and the flour—just as much as you need to make a nice, smooth dough—and knead thoroughly.

Cover the bowl with a damp cloth and leave the dough to rise in a warm place for about 1½ hours or until the dough has doubled in size. Then shape into loaves and prove for about 45 minutes. Bake in a hot oven for 30 minutes. Then turn the loaves round and finish them off in a moderate to cool oven for another 20 or 30 minutes.

This oatmeal dough makes the most delicious OATMEAL BUNS.

WALNUT BREAD
To make 2 medium-sized loaves.

INGREDIENTS
1 lb/450g white flour
8oz/225g wholemeal flour
½ oz/15g salt
1oz/25g sugar
4oz/110g butter or margarine
1 oz/25g fresh yeast
¾ pint/450ml warm milk, plus water if required
4 oz/110g walnut halves

METHOD
Put the flour, the sugar and the salt in a large bowl and mix thoroughly. Make a well. Pour in the yeast, creamed in a little of the milk, and the fat, warmed and liquid but not too hot, and the rest of the milk. Knead, adding warm water if required. Cover with a damp cloth and leave to rise in a warm place for 1½ hours or until the dough has doubled in size. Knock down the dough and knead in the walnut halves until they are evenly distributed throughout. Shape into loaves and prove for 45 minutes. Bake for 30 minutes in a hot oven, then turn the loaves round and finish them off in a moderate one for another 20 or 25 minutes.

BATH BUNS
To make about 18 medium-sized buns.

INGREDIENTS
1 lb/450g white flour
4oz/110g butter or margarine
1oz/25g fresh yeast
5 tablespoons milk
4oz/110g sugar

3 eggs
Small pinch of salt
4oz/110g sultanas
2oz/50g candied peel
A small quantity of crushed candy sugar, and 1 egg beaten with a
tablespoonful of milk

METHOD

Break the eggs into a bowl. Add the milk and the butter, warmed and
liquid but not hot, and whisk thoroughly.

Put the flour, the sugar and the salt in a large bowl and mix.
Make a well. Pour in the yeast, creamed in a little warm water. Pour
in the milk–butter–eggs mixture, and knead thoroughly. Cover the
bowl with a damp cloth and leave to rise in a warm place for 2
hours or until the dough has doubled in size. Then beat the dough
down and add the fruit and knead for a minute or two until evenly
distributed. Shape into oval buns and prove on a floured baking
sheet for 45 minutes. Brush them over with the egg and milk and
powder them with the crushed candy sugar and bake in a fairly hot
oven for about 30 minutes.

MUFFINS
To make 18 small muffins.

INGREDIENTS
1 lb/450g flour
½ pint/300ml milk
½ oz/15g fresh yeast
1 egg
1 teaspoonful salt
1oz/25g butter or margarine

Break the egg into a bowl. Add the milk and the butter, warmed and liquid but not too hot, and whisk.

Put the flour and the salt into a large bowl. Make a well and pour in the yeast, creamed in a little warm water. Add the butter-egg-milk mixture. Knead thoroughly, adding more flour or water as required, to make a soft dough that is not too sticky. Cover the bowl with a damp cloth and leave to rise in a warm place for about 1½ hours or until the dough has doubled in size.

Roll out the dough to a ½-inch/1.25cm thickness on a floured board. You will probably need more flour to sprinkle on the board and the dough to stop it from sticking. Cut the muffins out with a large tumbler. Punch any remains together and roll out and cut again until all the dough has been used.

The muffins should be baked right away on a griddle, being turned as soon as they're nicely browned on the bottom side. But if you've no griddle they will turn out very well if baked, without proving, on a baking sheet in a very hot oven with plenty of bottom heat and turned over after 6 or 7 minutes, and then given another 6 or 7 minutes.

CHELSEA BUNS

To make 18 buns.

INGREDIENTS

1 lb/450g white flour (scant)
4oz/110g butter or margarine
4oz/110g granulated sugar
1oz/25g fresh yeast
The zest of 1 lemon
2 eggs
4oz/110g currants
About 5 tablespoons milk
And 2 or 3 tablespoons of thick milk and sugar syrup

Break the eggs into a bowl. Add the milk and half the butter (liquid and cool) and whisk thoroughly.

Put the flour in a bowl with half the sugar and mix. Make a well. Pour in the yeast, creamed in a little warm water. Add the milk-eggs-butter mixture and the zest of one lemon (and more flour or milk as required to make a smooth, soft dough) and knead. Cover with a damp cloth and leave to rise in a warm place for 1½ hours or until the dough has doubled in size.

Then roll out the dough on a floured board into a thin strip about ¼-inch/6mm thick and about 3 times as long as it is wide. Spread the rest of the butter (softened, but not melted) over it. Sprinkle the currants and the rest of the sugar over the butter. Fold in the ends of the strip to make a square and roll out the other way into a strip the same size. Fold in the ends to make a square once more and then roll up the square like a Swiss roll. Cut into thick slices and put them on their sides, almost touching, on a floured baking sheet. Let them prove for 30 minutes and then bake them for 20 to 30 minutes in a fairly hot oven. Brush them heavily with the milk and sugar syrup when you have removed them from the oven.

CORNISH SPLITS
To make about 2 dozen.

INGREDIENTS
¼ pint/150ml milk
1oz/25g fresh yeast
4oz/110g butter or margarine
1 teaspoon salt
1 teaspoon sugar
1 lb/450g white flour

Warm the milk and dissolve the yeast in it. Add the sugar and salt and a few spoonfuls of flour, and stir. Leave to rise in a warm place until you can see that the yeast is working (bubbling).

Then add the flour and the butter, warmed and liquid but not too hot, and warm water, if required, to make a soft, smooth dough. Knead well. Cover with a damp cloth and leave to rise in a warm place for 1½ hours or until the dough has doubled in size.

Shape into small balls (about the size of a tangerine). Flatten the tops and bake, without proving, for about 20 minutes in a hot oven until golden brown.

Serve cold, split open, with clotted cream and strawberry jam.

TEA CAKES

PLAIN TEA CAKES (SALLY LUNN'S)
To make 4 large cakes.

INGREDIENTS
1 lb/450g white flour
¼ pint/150ml milk
4oz/110g butter or margarine
1oz/25g sugar
Large pinch of salt
1 egg
1oz/25g yeast

METHOD

Break the egg into a bowl and whisk in the milk and the butter, warmed and liquid but not too hot.

Put the flour in a large bowl with the sugar and the salt and mix. Make a well. Pour in the yeast, creamed in a little warm water. Add the milk-fat-egg mixture and knead thoroughly. Cover the bowl with a damp cloth and leave to rise in a warm place for 1½ hours until the dough has doubled in size.

Then beat the dough down and knead briskly for a few minutes. Roll out the dough on a floured board to a thickness of about ½ inch/1.25cm. Cut the cakes out with an upturned pudding basin and a knife. Let them prove on a floured baking sheet for 30 minutes.

With a sharp knife make four shallow cuts from the centre in each cake, to divide them into portions. And bake for about 20 minutes in a hot oven, turning them round after the first 10 minutes, until nicely browned. The cakes can be glazed by painting with a milk and sugar syrup as soon as they come out of the oven.

Ideally, these cakes should be made just in time for tea and sliced open as soon as they come out of the oven and buttered thickly and served hot.

They toast up very well.

FRUIT TEA CAKES

These can be made in exactly the same way as the Sally Lunn's, only when you knock the dough down after it has risen for the first time, knead in 2oz/50g currants, 2oz/50g sultanas and 2oz/50g of candied peel.

SPICE BUNS (WIGS)
To make 2 dozen wigs.

INGREDIENTS
1 lb/450g flour
2oz/50g butter or margarine
2oz/50g sugar
1 teaspoonful mixed spice
¼ oz/6g caraway seeds
½ oz/15g fresh yeast

½ pint/300ml milk
Pinch of salt

METHOD

Melt the fat and allow it to cool.

Put the flour the mixed spice, the caraway seeds, the sugar and the salt in a bowl and mix. Make a well. Pour in the yeast, creamed in a little warm water, and the milk. Knead thoroughly, adding more milk or flour if required to make a nice, smooth, soft dough. Roll out the dough on a floured board and cut into wedge-shaped buns. Put them on a floured baking sheet to prove for 30 minutes. Bake them for about 20 minutes in a hot oven, turning them round at half time.

(According to the *Encyclopaedia of Gastronomy*, 'A wigg was a wedge and these (Wigs) are wedge-shaped cakes'.)

SPICE BREAD

To make 2 small loaves.

INGREDIENTS
1 lb/450g flour
1oz/25g yeast
2oz/50g butter or margarine
Pinch of salt
2oz/50g sugar
2 teaspoons mixed spice
2oz/50g sultanas
2oz/50g currants
1oz/25g candied peel
About ½ pint/300ml milk

METHOD

Put the flour, the salt and the sugar in a large bowl and mix. Make a well. Pour in the yeast, creamed in a little of the milk. Add the spice, the rest of the milk and the butter, warmed and liquid but not too hot. Knead thoroughly. Cover the bowl with a damp cloth and leave to rise in a warm place for 1½ hours or until the dough has doubled itself.

Knock the dough down and knead in the fruit until it is all evenly distributed through the dough.

Shape the loaves and prove for 30 to 45 minutes. Bake for 30 to 45 minutes in a moderate or fairly hot oven, turning the loaves round at half time.

HOT CROSS BUNS
To make about 18 medium-sized buns.

INGREDIENTS
1 lb/450g flour
1oz/25g yeast
2oz/50g butter or margarine
2oz/50g moist sugar
2 large teaspoons mixed spice
(To make the best ever Hot Cross Buns, grind your own spice fresh)
1 egg
4oz/110g currants
2oz/50g candied peel
And about ½ pint/300ml milk

METHOD
If you want the buns for Good Friday breakfast make the dough some time on Thursday afternoon or evening.

Put the flour, the sugar, the salt and the spice in a large bowl and mix. Make a well. Pour in the yeast, creamed in a little of the milk. Add the egg and the butter, warmed and liquid but not too hot. Knead to a nice, clean, smooth dough (on the stiff side), using as much milk as you require. Then add the fruit and knead it evenly through the dough. Cover the bowl with a damp cloth and leave to rise overnight in the warmth of your kitchen (or for 2 hours, until the dough has doubled itself).

Knock the dough down and shape the buns and set them on a baking tray to prove for about 30 minutes. Mark the crosses on them with a paper knife or a blunt pointed pencil and bake in a hot oven for about 15 minutes (turning them round as necessary).

Brush them over with a thick milk and sugar syrup when they come from the oven, to glaze them.

MRS. BEETON'S YEAST CAKE
To make 1 good-sized cake.

INGREDIENTS
12oz/350g flour
¼ pint/150ml milk
2oz/50g butter or margarine
1oz/25g fresh yeast
2 eggs
4oz/110g moist sugar
6oz/175g currants
2oz/50g candied peel

METHOD
Melt the butter and put it in a bowl and allow to cool. Break in the eggs and pour in the milk and whisk to a froth.

Put the flour and sugar in a large bowl and mix. Make a well. Pour in the yeast, creamed in a very little warm water. Add the milk-butter-eggs mixture, and knead until you've made a nice smooth, soft dough. Then cover the bowl with a damp cloth and leave to rise in a warm place for at least 1½ hours, or until the dough has doubled itself.

Now add the fruit and knead well to make sure it's evenly distributed.

Line a cake tin with greaseproof paper and put in the dough. Let it prove for ½ hour. Bake for 30 minutes in a hot oven, then for about 1 hour in a moderate to cool oven.

DOUGHNUTS

(There are a whole host of doughnuts, English, American and Continental, but the following is a good, basic recipe.)

To make about 2 dozen medium-sized doughnuts.

INGREDIENTS
12oz/350g flour
1oz/25g yeast
¼ pint/150ml warm milk
2oz/50g butter or margarine, melted but cool
2 small eggs
2oz/50g sugar
Pinch of salt
Jam (e.g raspberry) and a little milk or egg for sealing—if you want to fill them
Some kitchen paper to lay them on for draining will be needed.
And a quantity of caster sugar to roll them in

METHOD
Dissolve the yeast in the warm milk. Beat in an ounce or two of the flour and leave covered in a warm place for 30 minutes.

Beat the egg, the sugar, the salt and the melted butter together with a whisk.

Join the two mixtures together and beat with the whisk. Then slap the rest of the flour gradually in with the fingers and hand. (A little more or a little less flour may be required—to make a soft, smooth dough, but not a sticky one.)

Cover with a damp cloth and leave to rise in a warm place for at least 1 hour.

Knock the dough down and knead for a few minutes.

Then, if you want to make filled doughnuts, roll little balls of the dough between the fingers. Flatten them with a rolling pin on a floured board. Put a teaspoonful of jam in the middle and fold up, sealing the edges with milk or egg.

If you want to make ring doughnuts, roll the dough out on the floured board and cut them out with a doughnut cutter. If you have no cutter you can use an upturned egg cup and a tumbler.

Or you can make doughnuts of whatever shape you fancy. The important thing to remember, though, is that they will swell up enormously as soon as they hit the fat in the frying pan so that all doughnuts must be made much smaller than one would at first imagine.

Set them to prove on a floured board or baking sheet, covered with a cloth, for about 15 minutes.

Fry them in deep boiling fat, turning them over as they get nicely browned on the underside. (They take about 7 or 8 minutes all together.)

Remove them and put them on paper to drain. Then roll them in the caster sugar. And the fresher—the warmer, almost—you serve them the better.

COFFEE BREADS FROM ABROAD

CROISSANTS (FRANCE)
To make about 2 dozen.

INGREDIENTS
¼ pint/150ml scalded milk
1oz/25g butter or margarine
1 heaped teaspoon salt
1½ tablespoons sugar
1oz/25g fresh yeast dissolved in a little warm water
12oz/350g flour (more or less)
4oz/110g butter or margarine
1 egg yolk, beaten with a little milk

METHOD: STAGE I
Put the 1oz/25g margarine or butter and the salt and sugar in a bowl. Pour the milk over, hot enough to melt the fat. Leave to cool to lukewarm and then add the dissolved yeast and stir. Add the flour,

gradually, and knead until the dough is soft, smooth and elastic. Cover the bowl with a damp cloth and put in a warm place to rise for two hours, or until the dough has doubled in size.

STAGE 2

Knock the dough down and put it in the refrigerator, or in a cold place, to chill thoroughly. Meanwhile wash the 4oz/110g butter or margarine by putting it in a large bowl of cold water and squeezing it between fingers until it is all soft and nicely spreadable.

STAGE 3

When the dough is chilled (after about 30 minutes in the fridge or 1 hour in the cold) roll it out on a floured board into a strip three times as long as it's wide. Spread the washed butter or margarine evenly over the strip and fold in the ends to form a square. Roll it out into another strip the same size—the other way—and fold in the ends to form a square and put it back in the fridge or in the cold place, to chill thoroughly again. Roll it out and fold twice more, at intervals of 30 minutes, and then leave it in the refrigerator or in the cold for an hour at the very least—or overnight, if you want croissants for breakfast. The dough will then be ready for shaping and baking.

STAGE 4. SHAPING

Roll the dough out on a floured board to ¼ inch/6mm thickness. Cut into 4-inch/10cm squares. Divide each square into 2 triangles. Roll each triangle up, starting at the longest base and rolling towards the apex, so that the pointed end is in the centre and underneath the roll. Shape into crescents and place on a lightly floured baking sheet.

STAGE 5. BAKING

Brush the croissants with the beaten egg yolk and milk and bake for 10 to 15 minutes (without proving) in a fairly hot or hot oven.

YEAST PUFF PASTE
To make a small quantity.

INGREDIENTS
1oz/25g fresh yeast
¼ pint/150ml lukewarm milk
2oz/50g sugar
2oz/50g butter or margarine, melted but cool
2 eggs, well beaten
Pinch of salt
12oz/350g flour
8oz/225g butter for spreading

METHOD
Dissolve the yeast in the milk. Add the sugar and salt and stir. Add enough flour to make a thin paste. Leave to rise in a warm place for 30 minutes or so.

Beat the melted butter with the eggs. Beat in the yeast-flour mixture. Gradually add the rest of the flour, slapping it in with the fingers. This must be a soft, smooth, elastic dough.

Leave to rise under a cloth in a warm place until doubled in size (1½ hours).

Wash the 8oz/225g butter by squeezing it between the fingers in a bowl of cold water until it is all soft and nicely spreadable. Then divide the butter in half and leave it in a bowl of cold water until you are ready for it.

Knock the dough together and roll it out on a floured board into a strip about ¼-inch/6mm thick and about three times as long as it is wide.

Shake one half of the butter dry and spread it over the centre third of the strip. Pull one end over, patting it down at the edges, and spread the rest of the butter over that. Pull the remaining end over and pat down the edges. Roll the dough out the other way into a strip the same size. Fold the ends in to make a square. Chill for half an hour in the refrigerator or for an hour in a cold place.

Roll it out again and fold in. Repeat this twice more at intervals of thirty minutes (rather longer if you have no refrigerator). Then allow the dough to rise for half an hour or so in moderate warmth.

The Yeast Puff Paste dough is ready for use.

DANISH PASTRY
Can be made with this dough

Roll out the dough on a floured board to ¼–inch/6mm thickness. Cut into shapes, as you fancy, fill with dried fruit, nuts, preserves jam, etc. Brush with a mixture of melted butter, egg and milk and bake (without proving) in a moderate oven for about 30 minutes.

When you take the pastries out of the oven you can either ice them or dust them with icing sugar.

SWEET CROISSANTS
Can be made with this dough

Roll out the dough to a thickness of ¼ inch/6mm on a floured board. Cut into 4-inch/10cm squares. Divide the squares into triangles and roll up as for Croissants. Brush with egg and milk and bake without proving for about 30 minutes in a moderate oven.

KOLATSCHEN (BOHEMIA)
Can be made with this dough

Roll out the dough on a floured board to ¼–inch/6mm thickness. Cut into small squares or circles according to fancy. Press down with your thumb in the centre of each so as to make a little indentation and fill the hole with jam, fruit, poppy seeds, nuts, sour milk cheese, whatever you like. Brush with melted butter, egg and milk mixture and bake, without proving, in a moderate or fairly hot oven for about 30 minutes. Dust with icing sugar.

And with this dough, of course, you can also make most of the things you can make with Puff Pastry. It is difficult to be over-enthusiastic about YEAST PUFF PASTE.

SWEET CROISSANTS (AUSTRIA)
To make about 2 dozen.

INGREDIENTS
1oz/25g fresh yeast
¼ pint/150ml lukewarm milk (scant)
2oz/50g sugar
Pinch of salt
4oz/110g butter or margarine
4 eggs
1 lb/450g flour (a little more may be needed)
The zest of 2 lemons
Egg and water, beaten, for brushing

METHOD
Dissolve the yeast in the milk. Add the sugar and salt and stir. Leave for a few minutes.

Melt the butter and allow to cool. Beat the eggs in with the butter, one after the other. Whisk till good and frothy.

Prepare the lemon zest.

Combine the yeast mixture, the lemon zest and the egg and butter mixture. Whisk. Gradually add the flour, slapping it in with the fingers, and knead until you have a soft, smooth dough.

Roll out the dough to a ¼-inch/6mm thickness on a floured board. Cut into 4-inch/10cm squares. Divide the squares into triangles and roll up as for ordinary croissants.

Prove on a lightly floured baking sheet for about 30 minutes. You don't want them to rise too much. Brush with the beaten egg and water and bake for 20 minutes in a fairly hot oven.

These sweet Croissants can be filled with jam or preserves if you like.

BRIOCHE (1)
To make about 18, in castle pudding tins.

INGREDIENTS
2oz/50g flour
1oz/25g fresh yeast
2 tablespoonfuls warm water
6oz/175g flour
3 eggs
6oz/175g melted butter (cool)
1 teaspoon salt
1 tablespoon sugar

METHOD
Cream the yeast in the warm water and mix with 2oz/50g flour. Put the little ball of dough into a bowl of warm water—where it will very quickly double in size and form a sponge on top of the water.

Put the 6oz/175g flour into a bowl and beat in the 3 eggs with your fingers. If too dry to beat add a little water. Beat for 5 or 10 minutes. Add the butter, salt and sugar and beat some more. Remove the yeast sponge from the water and mix it in with the batter. When everything seems truly blended together cover with a damp cloth and put in a warm place to rise for 2 or 3 hours. Then knock the dough down and leave in a cool place overnight.

In the morning the dough must be treated gently to keep the brioches as light as possible.

The dough can be baked as a cake in a ring mould, or in proper brioche tins (!) or in castle pudding tins. Half fill the tins with the dough, and allow to prove for 30 minutes. Bake in a hot oven; a ring loaf for about 30 minutes, castle pudding brioches for 15 or 20 minutes. If, after 10 or 15 minutes, the tops seem to be burning, you can either cover them with paper or bake a little longer at lower heat. If you're not sure whether they're baked or not you can always test them with a needle—like a cake.

BRIOCHE (2)
To make about 15 in castle pudding tins.

INGREDIENTS
8oz/225g flour
4oz/110g butter or margarine
2 eggs
1oz/25g yeast
1 teaspoon brandy
7 fl oz/200ml water
Pinch of salt
1 teaspoon sugar

METHOD
Crumble the yeast and mix it thoroughly (dry) with the flour in a bowl. Add the eggs, the sugar and the salt, and mix some more. Then pour in the butter, warmed and liquid but not too hot, and the water, to make a thick batter. Beat with a large spoon or with the fingers for 10 or 15 minutes or until the mixture begins to bubble. Stir in the brandy. Cover the bowl with a damp cloth and leave to rise in a warm place for at least 2 hours, or overnight.

Fill castle pudding tins (or proper brioche tins) half full with the mixture and bake (without proving), in a hot oven for about 15 minutes.

SWEET BRIOCHE—PANETTONE (ITALY)

To make 1 medium-sized cake or about a dozen small ones.

INGREDIENTS: STAGE 1
6oz/175g flour
1oz/25g yeast
¼ pint/150ml warm milk

METHOD
Cream the yeast in a little of the milk. Put the flour in a bowl. Make a well and pour in the yeast and the rest of the milk. Mix carefully and leave to rise in a warm place for 1½ hours.

INGREDIENTS: STAGE 2
6oz/175g flour
2oz/50g melted butter
3 egg yolks
Pinch of salt
2oz/50g sugar
3oz/75g stoned raisins
2oz/50g candied peel
Zest of 1 lemon
1 egg, beaten, for brushing

METHOD
Put this flour in another bowl and mix in the salt and the sugar. Then beat in the egg yolks and the fat with the fingers until the whole is nicely yellow. Now add the yeast dough (made in Stage 1) and knead thoroughly. You want a good stiff dough so if it's too wet add a little flour.

Lastly, add the raisins, the candied peel and the lemon zest, and knead until the fruit is evenly distributed through the dough.

Cover with a damp cloth and leave to rise overnight or until doubled in size (2 hours). Prove for 30 minutes in patty pans or on a well-greased baking sheet. And brush with beaten egg and bake for 10 to 15 minutes in a hot oven, then a further 10 or 15 minutes in a moderate oven.

APPLE CAKE—APFELKUCHEN (GERMANY)
To make 2 small cakes.

INGREDIENTS
1oz/25g fresh yeast
5 tablespoons warm milk
8oz/225g flour
1oz/25g butter or margarine
Zest of 1 lemon
1oz/25g sugar
1 egg, lightly beaten
Pinch of salt
Apples as required
Breadcrumbs or sugar for dredging and cinnamon and sugar for sprinkling over

METHOD
Dissolve the yeast in the warm milk. Mix in a little of the flour, enough to make a thin paste, and leave to stand in a warm place for 30 minutes.

Add the rest of the flour, the butter (warmed and liquid but not too hot), the lemon zest, the sugar, the egg and the salt.

Knead until the dough is quite smooth. Cover with a cloth and leave to rise for at least 1½ hours or until the dough has doubled in size.

Roll out on to well-greased tins (sponge cake tins are excellent for these cakes). Dredge with sugar or breadcrumbs. Peel apples, as required, and slice them thinly and arrange the slices prettily, overlapping, so as to cover the cake. Sprinkle with cinnamon and sugar and bake in a fairly hot oven for 15 to 20 minutes.

This same dough makes very good cakes with plums, prunes, dried apricots, what you will.

MILK STEAM CAKE (FRANCE)
To make 1 medium-sized cake.

INGREDIENTS
2oz/50g butter or margarine
5 tablespoons warm milk
1oz/25g fresh yeast
1oz/25g sugar
Pinch of salt
2 egg yolks
8oz/225g flour
To pour over: ¼ pint/150ml milk and 1oz/25g sugar
And some cinnamon and sugar

METHOD
Melt the butter. Pour it into a bowl and let it cool to lukewarm. Add the egg yolks, the sugar and the salt and the yeast, dissolved in the warm milk. Stir and mix until the sugar is dissolved.

Add the flour and knead until the dough is creamy and smooth. Then roll into a long sausage. Cut into ½-inch/1.25cm slices and put them into a well-greased baking pan. Cover the pan and let the cake rise for 45 minutes or until doubled in size. Then bake for about 15 or 20 minutes in a moderate or fairly hot oven, until light brown.

Meanwhile heat the ¼ pint/150ml milk and stir in the sugar.

Remove the cake from the oven as soon as it is nicely golden brown and pour over the hot milk and sugar. It will soak in immediately and the cake should rise high.

Sprinkle with the sugar and cinnamon and serve.

SAVARIN CAKE (FRANCE)

To make 1 small cake.

INGREDIENTS

1oz/25g yeast
5 tablespoons milk, warmed
4 eggs
Pinch of salt
1 heaped teaspoon sugar
2oz/50g butter
Small quantity of finely chopped almonds
2 tablespoons water, 2oz/50g sugar and 1 tablespoon rum—for the icing syrup
Whole blanched almonds and glacé cherries for decorating—as required

METHOD

Put the flour in a bowl. Make a well. Pour in the yeast dissolved in the warm milk. Beat in the eggs, one at a time, with your fingers until the dough is smooth. Cover the bowl with a damp cloth and leave in a warm place to rise for 1 hour, or until the dough has doubled itself.

Knock the dough down and add the sugar and the salt and butter (softened between the fingers but not melted). Beat and slap until the butter is all mixed in smoothly.

Butter a ring mould, or other suitable light cake tin, and dust heavily with the chopped almonds. Pour in the dough. Prove until it has doubled in size and bake for 20 minutes in a very hot oven, covering the cake with butter papers to stop the top from burning.

Meanwhile, make the syrup by gently boiling the water and sugar together (stirring continuously until the sugar is dissolved) for 10 minutes. Then add the rum and allow to cool a little.

As soon as the cake is out of the oven and removed from its mould and set upon its wire tray, spoon the syrup over it. Finally, decorate with the almonds and cherries.

EASTER BREAD (RUSSIA)

To make 1 medium-sized loaf.

INGREDIENTS
1oz/25g yeast
¼ pint/150ml warm milk
8oz/225g flour (more if required)
3oz/75g butter
3oz/75g sugar
3 egg yolks
4oz/110g candied peel
Pinch of salt

METHOD

Dissolve the yeast in the warm milk. Mix in a spoonful or so of the flour. Leave to rise for 30 minutes.

Beat the egg yolks, the salt, the sugar and the butter (warmed and liquid but not too hot) together.

Combine the two mixtures and with the fingers and hand beat in the rest of the flour. You want a soft, smooth dough. Add the peel. Cover with a damp cloth and leave to rise for 1½ hours, or until the dough has doubled itself.

Shape either into a long loaf or into a plait and prove on a lightly floured baking sheet for 30 minutes. Brush with beaten egg and milk and bake for 30 to 40 minutes in a moderate to fairly hot oven.

GUGELHUPF (AUSTRIA)

Almost any yeast cake, baked in the typical centre tube mould with the fluted wall, qualifies as a Gugelhupf. But the following is a very pleasant coffee cake, and if you have no proper mould an ordinary, plain, centre tube or ring mould will do very nicely.

To make 1 medium-sized cake.

INGREDIENTS
1oz/25g yeast
5 tablespoons warm milk
2oz/50g butter or margarine, melted but cool
2oz/50g sugar
2 eggs
8 oz/225g flour
The zest and juice of 1 orange
2oz/50g seedless raisins, soaked in a little water or rum
Breadcrumbs and icing sugar

METHOD

Dissolve the yeast in the warm milk. Mix in a spoonful or so of the flour and allow the mixture to rise for half an hour in a warm place.

Add, beating thoroughly or whisking after each addition, the butter, the eggs, the sugar, the orange juice and zest, and the raisins. And finally beat in the rest of the flour, gradually, slapping it in with the fingers.

This should be a very slack dough, that you can almost pour.

Grease the mould thoroughly and dust it with breadcrumbs.

Fill it half full with the dough. Let it rise for about an hour or until the dough has risen to the top of the mould. Then bake in a moderate oven for 30 to 40 minutes.

Let it cool on a wire rack and dust lightly with icing sugar to decorate.

STREUSEL CAKE (AUSTRIA)

Like the Gugelhupf recipe this is, as it were, a sample one. There must be hundreds of Streusel recipes.

To make 1 medium-sized cake.

INGREDIENTS 1. THE DOUGH

1oz/25g yeast

5 tablespoons milk

2 tablespoons sugar

Large pinch salt

2 eggs, well beaten

4oz/110g butter or margarine, melted and cooled

Zest of 1 lemon

About 8 oz/225g flour

2. THE STREUSEL.

1oz/25g butter

1oz/25g flour

6oz/175g sugar

1 tablespoon cinnamon powder

And you will need melted butter for brushing

METHOD

Dissolve the yeast in the lukewarm milk. Stir in the sugar and the salt and leave mixture to stand for a few minutes.

Beat in the eggs, the lemon zest and the butter. Gradually knead in the flour. Knead until very soft and smooth and elastic. Cover with a cloth and leave in a warm place to rise for 1½ hours.

Then knock down and roll out on a liberally floured baking pan—1 Swiss roll tin or two ordinary sponge tins will take this amount of dough nicely.

Prove for 30 minutes. And while the cake is proving prepare the streusel. Cut the ingredients together until they are crumbly.

Brush the top of the cake with melted butter and sprinkle heavily with the streusel. Bake in a moderate or fairly hot oven for about 30 minutes.

POPPY SEED BREAD (AUSTRIA)

To make 1 large loaf or several smaller ones—according to taste.

INGREDIENTS
1oz/25g yeast
¼ pint/150ml warm milk
2oz/50g sugar
1 teaspoonful salt
1 egg
About 12oz/350g flour
2oz/50g butter or margarine, melted and cooled
And 1 egg, beaten with water, for brushing, and a quantity of
poppy seeds

METHOD

Dissolve the yeast in the milk. Stir in the sugar and the salt. Leave to stand for a few minutes in moderate warmth. Add the egg, well beaten, and mix and add the flour and the butter and knead until you have a nice, smooth, creamy dough.

Leave to rise for 30 minutes or so. Then knock down and knead again for a few minutes. Leave to rise for 1½ hours or until the dough has doubled itself.

Then knock down and divide into three and plait (or make two or three smaller plaits). Prove until doubled in bulk.

Brush with egg and sprinkle heavily with poppy seed. Bake in a moderate oven for about 30 minutes (somewhat less if you have made 2 or 3 loaves).

SAFFRON BREAD (SWEDEN)
To make 1 large plait or 2 small.

INGREDIENTS
About 8oz/225g flour
¼ pint/150ml warm milk (scant)
1oz/25g fresh yeast
Large pinch of saffron. (It's expensive but a very little goes a very long way)
1oz/25g butter or margarine
2oz/50g sugar
1 egg
1 dessertspoon ground almonds
1oz/25g seedless raisins or 1oz/25g candied peel
And, for the topping: 1 egg; a quantity of granulated sugar; and some chopped nuts (almonds for preference)

METHOD
Dissolve the yeast in half the warm milk and mix in a little of the flour, enough to make a thin paste. Leave to rise in a warm place for 30 minutes.

Dry the saffron in a cool oven. Pound it with a little sugar. Then stir it in with the rest of the milk, and add it to the yeast mixture.

Whisk the butter, warm and liquid but not too hot, the egg and the rest of the sugar together. Work the butter-egg-sugar into the saffron-yeast mixture. Gradually beat in the flour, kneading briskly until you have a smooth soft dough, all of one good, yellow colour. Knead in the ground almonds and the raisins (plumped in water or rum). Cover with a cloth and leave to rise in a warm place for 1½ hours, or until the dough has doubled in size.

Knock the dough down and knead for a few minutes. Divide into 3 equal portions (or 6 if you want to make 2 plaits). Roll each out into a long, thin strand and plait.

Prove on a lightly floured baking sheet for about 30 minutes. Brush with beaten egg, sprinkle with chopped nuts and sugar. And bake for 20 to 30 minutes in a fairly hot oven.

STRIEZEL (AUSTRIA)

Apparently, there are about as many Striezels as there are provinces in Austria and Bohemia. The following is a recipe for a plain and simple Striezel—you can add nuts, fruit, candied peel, etc., as you fancy. But the important thing is the braiding.

To make one largish Striezel.

INGREDIENTS
2oz/50g fresh yeast
¼ pint/150ml milk
Pinch salt
4oz/110g sugar
1 whole egg and 1 egg yolk
4oz/110g melted butter or margarine (cool)
1 lb/450g flour—more as required
1 egg white beaten with a teaspoon of milk

METHOD

Dissolve the yeast in the milk. Add the sugar and the salt and stir until the sugar is all melted. Leave to stand in a warm place for 10 minutes or so—until the mixture starts to bubble.

Beat in the whole egg and the yolk. Beat in a little of the flour and the butter. Gradually work in the rest of the flour and knead to a stiff, clean dough. Cover with a damp cloth and leave to rise for an hour in a warm place.

Roll the dough out into a sausage. Cut into half. Cut one half into ¾ and ¼, and the other into ⅔ and ⅓; so that you have four pieces of dough ranging nicely in size.

Take the largest piece first. Divide into four and plait and lay it on a lightly floured baking sheet. Plait the next largest in three strands and place it on top of the first. Plait the third largest piece in three strands and put that on top of the second. Lastly, twist the smallest bit in two strands and put that on top of all. Press the whole down a little and shape gently but firmly into an oval.

Prove for 45 minutes or an hour, until the Striezel is about doubled in size. Brush with the egg white and milk and bake in a very hot oven for 15 minutes and then in a moderate oven for another 30 or 40 minutes.

SWEDISH COFFEE BREAD

To make one Coffee Twist, one Cinnamon Ring and about a dozen Fruit and Nut buns.

INGREDIENTS

1 lb/450g flour
8 fl oz/230ml lukewarm milk
1oz/25g fresh yeast
3oz/75g sugar
Pinch of salt
2oz/50g butter or margarine, melted and cool
1 egg for brushing
A quantity of chopped nuts, currants, sultanas and cinnamon powder. Sugar. About 1oz/25g melted butter or margarine

METHOD

Put the flour in a bowl. Add the sugar and salt and mix. Make a well. Pour in the yeast, creamed in a little of the milk, and the butter. Mix with a spoon until all the milk and fat have been absorbed. Then cover with a damp cloth and leave to rise in a warm place for 2 hours—or overnight, or until the dough has doubled in size.

Then knead the dough briskly until it is soft and smooth. Divide into 3 portions. You can make something different with each bit.

COFFEE TWIST

Take a third of the dough and divide into 3 equal portions. Roll each piece into a strand. Plait lightly and let the twist prove on a baking sheet for 45 minutes. Brush with beaten egg, sprinkle with sugar and chopped nuts and bake in a moderate oven for 15 to 20 minutes.

CINNAMON RING

Take a third of the dough and roll out as thinly as possible on a floured board. Brush with melted butter and sprinkle heavily with sugar and cinnamon. Roll up like a Swiss roll and join the ends together to make a ring. Brush the ends with beaten egg to make sure they seal. Put the ring on a baking sheet to prove. Decorate by cutting roll with scissors and pulling the leaves thus formed to alternate sides. Prove for 45 minutes. Brush with beaten egg and bake in a moderate oven for 15 to 20 minutes.

FRUIT AND NUT BUNS

Take the remaining third of the dough and roll out as thinly as possible on the floured board. Brush with melted butter and sprinkle heavily with sugar, currants, sultanas and chopped nuts. Roll up like a Swiss roll and cut into small buns. Decorate each bun with scissors according to your fancy. Prove on a baking sheet for 45 minutes. Brush with egg and bake in a hot oven for 5 or 10 minutes.

This Swedish Coffee Bread is a wonderful example of the joys of baking with yeast. The making of the dough is simple and trouble-free and if you don't want to use it all at one moment, you can leave it. You could start the dough off one evening before going to bed—5 or 10 minutes labour, less perhaps—and the following day, without much additional labour, you could have a fresh-baked Coffee Twist for breakfast, a fresh-baked Cinnamon Ring with your coffee after lunch, and fresh baked Fruit and Nut buns for tea!

A MISCELLANY

CHALLAH (JEWISH SABBATH BREAD)
To make one small Challah.

INGREDIENTS
8oz/225g flour
1 teaspoon salt
1 teaspoon sugar
2oz/50g vegetable fat melted, and cool
5 tablespoons warm water (approx.)
1oz/25g yeast
1 egg
Pinch of saffron
A quantity of poppy seeds and the yolk of an egg, beaten

METHOD
Dry the saffron in a cool oven, pound with the sugar. Dissolve the
yeast in the warm water. Combine the yeast water and the saffron

sugar and stir.

Put the flour in a bowl and make a well. Pour in the yeast-saffron, the fat and the egg, lightly beaten. Add the salt and knead to a good, clean, stiff dough. Adding more water if necessary. Cover with a damp cloth and leave in a warm place to rise for 1½ hours or until the dough has doubled itself.

Knock the dough down and divide into 3, 5 or 7 and plait—the knobblier the loaf is the better.

Let it prove on a lightly floured baking sheet in moderate warmth for 45 minutes. Brush with egg yolk and sprinkle heavily with poppy seeds and bake—for about 15 minutes in a hot oven, and then another 45 minutes in a moderate oven.

COULIBIAC (RUSSIA)

INGREDIENTS
¼ pint/150ml milk
4oz/110g flour
½oz/50g yeast
3 eggs
4oz/110g butter, margarine or lard, melted and cooled
8oz/225g to 12oz/350g flour
1 dessertspoon salt
1 egg yolk for brushing
And the filling. Meat, fish, mushrooms, olives, hard-boiled eggs, etc.

METHOD
Dissolve the yeast in the milk which should be lukewarm. Add the 4oz/110g flour and beat till smooth. Leave to rise for 30 minutes. Add the eggs, the salt, the fat and the flour as required to make a soft, smooth dough. Knead thoroughly. Cover with a cloth and leave to rise in a warm place for 1½ hours or until the dough has doubled itself.

A MISCELLANY

Prepare the filling.

Roll the dough out in a square on a floured board to a thickness of about ¼ inch/6mm. Put the filling in layers in the middle. Wrap the dough up round the filling like wrapping up a parcel (seal the joins with egg or milk). Make two steam vents in the top. Paint with egg yolk and bake (without proving) in a hot oven for 40 to 50 minutes.

CARAWAY SEED BREAD (1) (SWEDEN)
To make 1 medium-sized loaf.

INGREDIENTS
2oz/50g moist brown sugar
¼ pint/150ml water
1 dessertspoon caraway seeds
Zest of 1 orange
1oz/25g butter or margarine
Small pinch salt
1oz/25g yeast dissolved in a little warm water
8oz/225g to 12oz/350g flour. (Half of which can be rye flour, if you like)

METHOD
Boil the sugar, the water, the orange zest, the butter and the caraway seeds for about 3 minutes. Let the mixture cool to lukewarm. Add the salt, the dissolved yeast and 4oz/110g of the flour. Beat until smooth. Cover with a cloth and leave to rise in a warm place until doubled in size (1½ hours).

Knead in as much of the remaining flour as is required to make a nice, smooth dough. Half fill a large bread tin with the dough and prove for 45 minutes. Bake in a moderate oven for 45 minutes or 1 hour.

CARAWAY SEED BREAD (2)
To make 1 medium-sized loaf

INGREDIENTS
¼ pint/150ml lukewarm milk
2oz/50g butter or margarine, melted but cool
2oz/50g sugar
Teaspoon salt
1oz/25g yeast
1 tablespoon caraway seeds
8oz/225g to 12oz/350g flour

METHOD
Dissolve the yeast in the milk. Add the sugar, the salt and a spoonful or two of the flour and beat until smooth. Leave to rise for 20 minutes or so.

Put most of the flour in a bowl. Mix in the caraway seeds. Make a well. Pour in the yeast mixture and the fat and knead, adding more flour if required, until you have a good, smooth, stiff dough. Cover with a cloth and leave to rise in a warm place for 1½ hours, or until the dough has doubled itself.

Shape into a long roll and prove on a lightly floured baking sheet for 30 to 45 minutes. Bake for 45 to 55 minutes in a moderate oven.

PIZZA (ITALY)
To make 1 medium-sized pizza, enough for 4 persons.

INGREDIENTS: THE DOUGH
8oz/225g flour
1oz/25g yeast dissolved in a little warm water
1 tablespoon olive oil
1 heaped teaspoon salt
Warm water as required

THE FILLING:

(the following is for Pizza Alla Napolitana, but of course there are many different sorts of Pizza and almost you can use what you fancy)

1 lb/450g tomatoes
1 clove garlic, chopped
2oz/50g grated Parmesan cheese
1 small tin fillets of anchovy
Marjoram
Salt and pepper
Oil for frying

METHOD: THE DOUGH

Put the flour in a bowl and beat in the salt and the olive oil. Make a well. Pour in the yeast and the olive oil and water as required to make a nice, smooth, softish dough. Cover with a cloth and leave to rise in a warm place for 1½ hours or overnight or until suppertime, etc.

THE FILLING

Remove the skins of the tomatoes and chop. Fry them in a pan with the olive oil and garlic. Add the cheese and the anchovies just before the tomatoes are ready. Add salt and pepper and a sprig of marjoram and simmer for 20 to 30 minutes.

Now roll the dough out on to a well-greased baking tin. Cover with the filling and bake (without proving) for 15 to 20 minutes in a hot oven.

RUM BABA (FRANCE)

To make a dozen small babas (castle pudding tin size) or one largish baba.

INGREDIENTS
4oz/110g flour
1oz/25g yeast
5 tablespoons milk
2 eggs
2oz/50g butter or margarine (softened but not melted)
Pinch of salt
2oz/50g sugar
1oz/25g candied peel
1oz/25g currants and 1oz/25g seedless raisins, plumped in a little rum
For the syrup—4oz/110g sugar
3 tablespoons water
1 tablespoon rum

METHOD

Dissolve the yeast in the warm milk and add to the flour. Beat in the 2 eggs, slapping with the fingers until the whole is smooth and of uniform colour. Cover with a cloth and leave to rise in a warm place for 45 minutes.

Add the sugar, the salt and the softened butter and beat, slapping with fingers, until all is mixed and smooth. Then add the fruit and mix thoroughly.

To make one large baba—pour the mixture into a well-buttered ring mould or other light cake tin. Half fill the mould. Prove until doubled and bake in a hot oven for 45 minutes, covering the top with butter papers to stop it burning if necessary.

To make small babas—half fill well-buttered castle pudding tins with the mixture. Prove until doubled and bake in a hot oven for about 15 minutes.

Remove the cakes from their tins (if they don't slip out easily wrap them up in cloths for 10 minutes or so) and let them cool on a wire rack.

Make the syrup—boil the water and sugar gently together for 10 minutes, then remove from heat and add the rum, stirring all the time.

Pour the syrup over the large baba. Or dip the small ones into it.

SALT STICKS (AUSTRIA)
To make 3 to 4 dozen.

INGREDIENTS
1oz/25g yeast
¼ pint/150ml lukewarm milk
2oz/50g butter or margarine, melted but cool
1 teaspoon each sugar and salt
About 8oz/225g flour
Poppy seeds and salt

METHOD
Dissolve the yeast in a little of the milk and leave to stand.

Put the rest of the milk, the butter, the salt and the sugar in a bowl. Make sure it's not too hot. Stir in the yeast and leave to stand until it bubbles.

Beat in the flour gradually—as much as is required. And knead to a soft, smooth dough. Cover with a damp cloth and leave to rise 1½ hours.

Knock the dough together and roll out on a floured board to ¼-inch/6mm thickness, or thinner. Cut into 4-inch/10cm squares. Divide the squares into two triangles. Roll up each triangle as for a croissant, but don't shape into crescents, leave them straight.

Prove on a lightly floured baking sheet for 15 minutes. Brush with water and sprinkle with salt and poppy seeds and bake for 10 to 15 minutes in a hot oven.

If you make them very small they go well served with drinks.

CAKES AND BISCUITS
INTRODUCTION

Tea seems to be the meal which is most often ignored by connoisseurs of good food. Perhaps this is because afternoon tea is a feminine meal and many connoisseurs are men, or perhaps it is because you cannot drink wine at tea. . . . Whatever the reason, it seems to me to be a pity, because tea is the one meal which still retains, at its best, a distinctly British flavour and also because it is a meal at which the food is judged by much the same standards by people of all walks of life in this country. A menu saying 'home-made cakes, bread and jam' arouses the same expectations of excellence in us all, whereas one saying that 'the pâté is made by the proprietor himself' would leave many people cold. (That both notices might be equally misleading, does not alter the fact that more people would be aware that they had been misled by the first.)

Tea, in order to become a meal in its own right, must include a cake or cakes. A cup of tea and a slice of bread and butter or a biscuit is not a meal, it is a snack. No cake for tea is a dismal thing and reminiscent of juvenile punishments. Yet it is all too easy for a busy mother to produce her favourite cake so often that finally it grows stale long before it is finished. I have therefore included some recipes in this book which are economical or quick to prepare, or both, in the hope that something new can be put on the family table without too much trouble to the cook.

Apart from their function at tea, cakes can make an admirable finish for a luncheon or dinner. In their more exquisite versions they would not disgrace the most fastidious menu and they have the advantage for most hostesses of being preparable well in advance. It is a pity that some restaurants which excel at main dishes descend to tinned fruit and mass-produced ice-cream for dessert. They would do better to produce a really good cake which would round off the meal with a touch of individuality.

I have included some biscuits and pastries in this little book because very often the dividing line between them and cakes is hard to draw anyway. It is a pleasant contrast to have biscuits as well as cakes on the tea-table and a tin of home-made biscuits is always useful. Many of them keep admirably in an airtight tin and they are a stand-by for unexpected visitors or for days when there just isn't enough time to make a cake.

I have tried to divide the cakes into sections according to their main ingredients. Many people have their favourite flavours and it seems the simplest way for people to find what cake they can make with the ingredients in their store cupboard. However, as very many cakes are based on two basic recipes, the fatless sponge and the plain creamed mixture, I have given my favourite recipes for these two in the opening chapter, with a few suggestions on varying the flavour. The ingenious cook will, of course, be able to think of many more.

I would like to apologize to natives of those countries whose recipes I may have borrowed. Such delicate and delicious things undergo a sea change when they are produced by an alien cook. I can only plead that I've written them down here because the results have proved popular with my own family and friends and that they are the nearest I can get to the original.

BASIC CAKES

A great many cakes are variations on two basic methods: the fatless sponge and the plain creamed mixture.

Most people have their favourite recipe for a PLAIN CAKE (the plain creamed mixture) and here is mine.

INGREDIENTS
6oz/175g butter
6oz/175g sugar
4 eggs
8oz/225g flour
2 teaspoons baking-powder
Pinch of salt
Milk to mix

METHOD
Cream the fat and sugar together until they are really soft like whipped cream. This doesn't take very long if you cut up the butter

and warm it first—but don't 'oil' the butter. Separate the whites and yolks of the eggs. Beat the yolks, one at a time, into the butter and sugar mixture. Sieve the flour, salt and baking-powder together several times. If you want to mix in the baking-powder properly this is really necessary. If you use a recipe in which cocoa and flour are sieved together you will see that several sievings are needed before the cocoa is evenly distributed, and the same applies to baking-powder. Then whisk the egg whites until they are fairly firm but not stiff and dry, Fold the flour into the sugar-butter-egg mixture, and finally fold in the egg white and add enough milk to make a 'dropping mixture'—probably about half a teacupful. Try to avoid beating the mixture, just turn it gently, over and over, but flour, egg whites and milk should all be thoroughly mixed in. Put into a well-buttered cake tin—with greaseproof paper at the bottom, this will make it much easier to turn out—and bake in a moderate oven (300°F, Gas mark 2) for about 1 hour.

Do use butter if you possibly can. It will only add a few pence on to the cost of the cake and it will make all the difference to the flavour. If not, use half butter and half margarine, or half margarine and half lard. Margarine by itself is often not 'fatty' enough.

Here is my basic recipe for a

FATLESS SPONGE

INGREDIENTS
4 eggs
the weight of the 4 eggs in caster or
icing sugar
the weight of 3 eggs in flour
1 tablespoon full of lemon juice or
warm water

I use the eggs to weigh the other ingredients because proportions are important in a sponge and eggs vary in size.

Sieve the flour once or twice to make sure there are no lumps and that it is well aerated.

Separate the whites and the yolks of the eggs.

Beat the yolks of the eggs with the sugar until they become thick and pale in colour. This will take some time but it is very important not to stint your labours on this part of the operation!

Whisk the egg whites until they are stiff but not too dry.

Fold the flour bit by bit into the egg yolk-sugar mixture. Use a metal spoon and make sure there are no bits of dry flour left—but don't beat the mixture.

Fold in the egg whites, again making sure that they are thoroughly mixed in. Finally, stir in the lemon juice or hot water very gently.

The mixture should be spongy and yet fairly runny. Divide into sandwich tins which have been well greased and had caster sugar lightly shaken all over them—put a little sugar into each tin and shake it all over.

Bake in a fairly hot oven, 350° to 400°F, for about 25 minutes.

A wire whisk is really the best thing to beat with because it does aerate the mixture better than a rotary whisk. I find this takes a long time so I cheat and start off with the rotary whisk and complete my beating with the wire one—this seems to work pretty well.

Both these recipes are open to as many variations as you have ideas, but remember, if you use other dry ingredients, like cocoa or ground almonds then you must subtract the weight of these ingredients from the amount of flour used.

As this is a chapter on basics I would like to add a note on flavourings. Please try not to use so-called 'essences'! Lemon or orange flavouring is best got from the grated rinds of the fruits themselves. Vanilla pods give a far more delicate flavour than the commercial essence. They are rather expensive to buy, but do try them as they are not at all extravagant in use. Keep a jar of caster sugar and one of icing sugar with a vanilla pod buried in each. The pods will flavour the sugar and if you keep the jars filled up the pods will continue to do their job for many weeks.

If you do use commercial essences then please use them sparingly. Too much flavouring is worse than too little if your other ingredients are good.

Keep one or two miniature bottles of liqueurs in your store cupboard. Brandy and rum are especially useful. And then you can add a touch of luxury to otherwise plain cakes.

FRUIT CAKES

Cakes made with dried fruits are generally good keepers. Some of the richer ones are all the better for keeping. They are excellent for picnics as they are usually firm in texture and not sticky to eat.

Here is one of the favourites in our family. It is much more economical to make than many fruit cakes and it has a rather unusual flavour because of the demerara sugar. It is called:

BOODLES CLUB CAKE

INGREDIENTS
8oz/225g butter
8oz/225g demerara sugar
8oz/225g raisins (sultanas will do but
raisins give a better flavour)
2 eggs

1 lb/450g flour
2 teaspoons bicarbonate of soda
¼ pint/150ml milk

METHOD

Cream the butter and sugar. Beat in the eggs. Stir in the flour mixed with the dried fruit.

Dissolve the bicarbonate of soda in the milk which should be slightly warmed, and beat this mixture into the other ingredients and mix really well.

Bake in a moderate oven for about 3 hours in a lined tin.

This makes a large cake—but the quantities can easily be halved.

ECONOMY FRUIT CAKE

This is a huge cake, economical to make and a good keeper. It isn't particularly luscious but it's just the thing if you are facing a weekend with lots of young people with hearty appetites. You need a very big tin to bake it in. Use a measuring jug for all the ingredients.

INGREDIENTS

½ pint/300ml sugar
½ pint/300ml melted butter or margarine
½ pint/300ml strong coffee
2 eggs
1 teaspoon mixed spice
9 fl oz/250ml sultanas
grated rind of an orange
2 pints/1.2 litres flour
½ pint/300ml golden syrup
2 level dessertspoons baking-powder

METHOD

Beat up the eggs and sugar until pale and fluffy. Sift the flour and baking-powder together. Add all the ingredients to the eggs and sugar mixture, stirring in the flour and sultanas last. Turn into a large greased and floured tin (a 9 inch/23cm cake-tin or a roasting-tin) and bake in a moderate oven (350°F) for just under an hour.

SPONGE FRUIT CAKE
This is much lighter than the average fruit cake.

INGREDIENTS
5oz/150g seeded raisins
2oz/50g shelled walnuts
7oz/200g flour
1 teaspoon cinnamon
1 teaspoon lemon juice
4oz/110g butter
7oz/200g caster sugar
yolks of 3 eggs and 1 white
1 level teaspoon bicarbonate of soda
pinch of salt

METHOD
Chop the raisins and walnuts coarsely. Put them in a basin and pour over them the bicarbonate of soda dissolved in a breakfast-cup full of boiling water. Leave them to stand while you sift the flour with the salt.

Cream the butter and sugar (if possible flavoured with vanilla). Beat the egg yolks and the white thoroughly and add them to the creamed mixture. Stir in the cinnamon and lemon juice and then stir in the flour alternately with the fruit and nuts. Do not beat but mix well.

Bake in a large loaf-tin in a very moderate oven (335°F, Gas mark 3) for 1¼ hours. Cool in the tin for 5 minutes before turning it out.

CHRISTMAS CAKE

This is the Christmas Cake I make every year for our family. None of us like icing so I just arrange some blanched almonds on the top of the cake before putting it in the oven. Make it several weeks before you need it. And if you do like icing start work on it two days before you intend to eat it.

Cover it with a layer of almond icing and cover this with a layer of water icing. When this is dry cover it with royal icing and allow this to dry overnight in a warm room before you start to decorate. Allow another twelve hours for the decorations to dry out, also. If you don't like almond icing, start with the water icing which will give a smooth surface to the cake.

INGREDIENTS
12oz/350g butter
1 lb/450g sultanas
8oz/225g chopped peel
1 lb/450g flour
1 lb/450g raisins
6 eggs
1 lb/450g sugar
8oz/225g ground almonds
a little nutmeg and mixed spice
the juice of a lemon
½ wineglass brandy

METHOD
Rub the butter into the flour and sugar, add the fruit and other dry ingredients. Beat the eggs and add them to the mixture with the brandy and the lemon juice. Mix very well. Line a 9 inch/23cm tin and bake in a very slow oven for about 8 hours.

BISHOP'S BREAD

This is my version of the Austrian cake known as Bischofsbrot. It is extravagant but rich and very delicious. It is unusual in having grated chocolate in it.

INGREDIENTS
2 eggs, and their weight in butter, flour and sugar
2oz/50g raisins
2oz/50g almonds, or other nuts
2oz/50g chocolate
2oz/50g candied peel

METHOD
Separate the egg yolks and whites. Chop the chocolate and nuts.

Cream the butter with half the sugar. Add the egg yolks and cream well.

Whisk the egg whites until stiff, then whisk in the rest of the sugar.

Fold the egg whites into the butter–sugar mixture alternately with the flour. Add the other ingredients gradually.

Bake in an oblong tin in a moderate oven (360°F, Gas mark 4) for about 45 minutes.

FRENCH PLUM CAKE

INGREDIENTS
6oz/175g sugar
6oz/175g butter
4oz/110g seeded raisins
2oz/50g currants
2oz/50g mixed cut peel
4 eggs
11oz/280g flour
2 teaspoons baking-powder
1 tablespoon rum

METHOD

Cream the sugar and the butter. Add the dried fruit and the eggs, one by one. Beat well after adding each egg. Sift the flour and the baking-powder together and fold into the mixture. Add the rum and then beat thoroughly. Line a large bread-tin with waxed paper and fill it three-quarters full with the batter. Bake for 45 to 50 minutes in a warm oven, 375°F, Gas mark 4.

SCOTCH SEED CAKE

INGREDIENTS
8oz/225g flour
8oz/225g butter
8oz/225g sugar
2oz/50g almonds (bitter if possible)
4oz/110g orange peel
2½ oz/65g citron peel
5 eggs
½ a grated nutmeg
½ teaspoon caraway seeds
½ wineglass brandy

METHOD

Cream the butter and sugar. Beat the eggs well and add them to the mixture bit by bit alternately with the flour. Add all the other dry ingredients, except the caraway seeds, and finally, stir in the brandy. Pour into a well-lined cake-tin. Sprinkle the caraway seeds on top and bake in a moderate oven, 340°F, Gas mark 3. Avoid moving the cake until it is nearly done.

DUNDEE CAKE

INGREDIENTS
10oz/275g flour
4oz/110g currants
4oz/110g raisins
4oz/110g sultanas
4oz/110g mixed chopped peel
3oz/75g ground almonds
2oz/50g whole almonds
grated rind of 1 orange
5 eggs
8oz/225g butter
8oz/225g sugar
Pinch of salt

METHOD
Cream the butter and the sugar. Add the eggs and sieved flour alternately, beating well. Add the fruit, ground almonds, the grated orange rind, and the salt. Turn into a well-greased and lined tin. Cover the top with the almonds (which may be split first) and bake in a slow oven, 300°F, Gas mark 2, for 2½ hours.

CHOCOLATE CAKES

Chocolate is one of the favourite cake flavours. It's well worth keeping some plain chocolate in your store cupboard for use in making cakes. These range from quite economical ones to the most extravagant and delicious concoctions. All of them are improved by being served with whipped cream. And chocolate goes very well with coffee so that any chocolate cake can be served as dessert.

If you have no plain chocolate in the house you can substitute cocoa in those recipes in which the chocolate is melted first. Mix the cocoa with a little milk and stir over heat into a smooth, thick paste. You will not need as much cocoa as chocolate—about half the quantity—and you may find you need a little more sugar—but this is a question of taste.

I start with a cake I make very often because it is quick and economical and also a good keeper. In fact, it improves if not cut for a day or two. It is called:

CHOCOLATE MANITOU

INGREDIENTS
3oz/75g plain chocolate
1 teacup milk
1½ teacups flour
3oz/75g butter
3oz/75g sugar
1 egg
2 teaspoons baking-powder
1 teaspoon bicarbonate of soda
vanilla pod or essence

METHOD
Melt the chocolate in the milk with a piece of vanilla pod and one ounce (25g) of the butter. Stir over a gentle heat until the chocolate is quite melted. Cut up the rest of the butter in a mixing-bowl and pour over the hot chocolate mixture after removing the vanilla pod. Stir until the butter has melted.

Then stir in the sugar and the egg. Beat in the flour and, lastly, add the baking-powder and the bicarbonate. Beat thoroughly—a wire whisk is best.

Pour into a well-greased tin and bake in a moderate oven, 350°F, Gas mark 4, for about 45 minutes.

(If you have no vanilla pod, add a half teaspoonful of vanilla essence when you put in the egg and the sugar.)

DEVIL'S FOOD CAKE

INGREDIENTS
8oz/225g flour
½ teaspoon bicarbonate of soda
1½ teaspoons baking-powder
8oz/225g sugar
1 teaspoon salt
4oz/110g butter
4 tablespoons sour cream or milk
2 tablespoons hot milk
3oz/75g chocolate
2 eggs
vanilla pod or essence

METHOD
Dissolve the chocolate in the hot milk with a piece of vanilla pod. Sift together the flour, soda, baking-powder, salt and sugar. Stir in the sour cream and the butter (melted but not hot). Add the milk and chocolate mixture, after allowing it to cool and having removed the piece of vanilla pod. Fold in the lightly beaten eggs (and vanilla essence if the pod is not available, ½ teaspoon). Beat for a few minutes and then turn out into two well-greased 8 inch/20cm sandwich-tins. Bake for 30 minutes in a moderate oven, 350°F, Gas mark 4. Sandwich together with chocolate filling, and top with icing if you like.

PANAMA CAKE

This cake must be made in a tin with a loose bottom, and if possible in a spring-sided tin. It's practically impossible to turn it out of an ordinary tin without breaking it—though it can be stuck together afterwards with the filling and still taste delicious!

INGREDIENTS

3 eggs

2½oz/65g icing sugar

2oz/50g chocolate

2½oz/65g almonds

Do not blanch the almonds but grate them finely or put them through a food mill. Grate the chocolate and mix it with the almonds. Separate egg yolks and whites. Whisk egg yolks and 2oz (50g) of the sugar until thick and creamy.

In Austria, where this cake comes from, the cook may beat for half an hour. If you cannot face doing this you must be content with a less than perfect cake.

Whip egg whites until stiff, fold in remaining sugar, and whisk again until smooth. Fold egg whites into egg yolk mixture alternately with grated almonds and chocolate.

Bake in a buttered and floured tin in a moderate oven, 350°F, Gas mark 4, for about 1 hour.

When the cake is cold, cut it once or twice and fill it with the following cream:

Melt 1oz (25g) chocolate over hot water. Cream 2½ oz (65g) butter with 2½ oz (65g) icing sugar, and add the melted chocolate which should not be too hot. Beat well and then beat in an egg. Beat this mixture until it is thick and creamy.

Keep enough of the cream to cover the top and sides of the cake. Then sprinkle it with chopped, roasted almonds.

RICH CHOCOLATE CAKE

INGREDIENTS
8oz/225g chocolate
8oz/225g butter
2oz/50g ground rice
6oz/175g caster sugar
4oz/110g flour
4 eggs
1 teaspoon baking-powder
vanilla pod or essence
a little milk

METHOD
Melt the chocolate in a little milk with a piece of vanilla pod. Cream the butter and sugar, add chocolate when cool. Separate the whites and yolks of the eggs.

Add the yolks one at a time to the butter and sugar mixture, beating each one in. Beat in the flour, rice and baking-powder, well-sieved together. Whisk the egg whites stiff and fold them in. Put the mixture into a well-greased and lined tin and bake in a moderate oven, 325°F, Gas mark 3, for 1¼ hours.

GIPSY SLICES

INGREDIENTS
2 eggs
2oz/50g sugar
2oz/50g flour
1oz/25g chocolate
½ oz/15g butter

Grate or break the chocolate and put it in a bowl with the butter. Put it in a warm place to soften. Put the eggs and sugar in a bowl over steam and whisk until thick and creamy. Remove from heat and go on beating until cool. Fold in the sieved flour, and finally the softened butter and chocolate. Put a piece of buttered greaseproof paper on to a baking-sheet, and spread the mixture on it about ½ inch/1.25cm thick. Bake until firm to the touch in a hot oven, 400°F, Gas mark 6.

Remove paper while still hot. Cut into slices when cool and fill with the following cream:

Put 2oz (50g) grated chocolate into a saucepan with ¼ pint (150ml) cream. Bring slowly to the boil stirring all the time. Allow to boil up once and then remove from the fire and pour into a bowl. Stir until cool. Chill thoroughly and then whisk gently until thick.

Real cream is essential and this is a most delicious filling. You can of course fill the slices with chocolate butter icing but they will not then be the genuine article.

Here are two extravagant and delicious cakes for which I give rather large quantities as they are really party pieces.

DOBOS TORTE

INGREDIENTS
6 eggs
5oz/150g icing sugar
4oz/110g flour

METHOD
Sift the flour. Separate the egg yolks and whites. Whisk the egg yolks with half the sugar until thick and creamy. Whip the egg whites until stiff and then fold in the remaining sugar. Fold the egg whites into

the yolks alternately with the flour.

Spread buttered and floured cake-tins with a thin layer of the mixture. This quantity should be enough for five or six layers, and they are most easily baked in tins with removable bottoms. Remember that the filling should be as thick as the cake, so keep the layers thin! Bake in a warm oven, 375°F, Gas mark 5, for about 15 minutes or until pale gold.

When all the layers are cold put them one on top of the other with waxed paper in between each, cover with a board and a weight and weigh them down. Leave them like this while you prepare the filling.

For this you require:

4 eggs
4oz/110g icing sugar
4oz/110g chocolate
4oz/110g butter
2oz/50g ground roasted hazelnuts

Soften the chocolate in a bowl over hot water. When soft, remove from the heat, stir a little and then add the sugar and the eggs. Replace over steam and whip until thick and creamy. Remove from heat and whip until cool. Cream the butter, then add the chocolate cream, very gradually, beating in each addition really well. Finally, stir in the roasted nuts.

Now take your pastry layers from under their weight, trim them and spread them with the cream, keeping back one pastry layer.

Place this spare round on a lightly floured board. Melt 3oz/75g lump sugar over gentle heat, stirring all the time, and continue cooking until it is pale golden in colour. Remove from the fire and spread over the spare pastry round. Mark into slices with a buttered knife. This has to be done very quickly before the caramel hardens. If you find it does get hard, you can put the board with the pastry on it into a very low oven for a few seconds to soften it again.

Put this caramelled pastry on top of the other layers, and cover the sides with the remaining cream.

And here is a cake which is not cooked. It is very rich and should be served in very thin slices.

ITALIAN UNCOOKED CHOCOLATE CAKE

INGREDIENTS
6oz/175g butter
6oz/175g cocoa
6oz/175g ground almonds
6oz/175g Petit Beurre biscuits
6oz/175g sugar
1 egg
1 egg yolk
1 tablespoon very strong coffee

METHOD
Melt the sugar over a very low heat in the coffee. Cream the butter and mix in the cocoa and ground almonds. Cool the sugar syrup a little and then add to the creamed mixture. Beat well. Beat the whole egg and the yolk together and stir them into the mixture. And lastly fold in the biscuits which have been broken into small pieces or roughly crumbled.

Lightly oil an oblong or square tin—a bread-tin is a good shape—and press the mixture down into it. Leave in a cold place overnight before turning out.

NUT CAKES

Nut cakes are especially delicious. There are the kind most usually met with in this country with the nuts coarsely chopped and mixed into a plain cake mixture, and there are also those, more popular on the Continent, with the nuts ground finely and added to the cake in place of flour. For quite a number of these latter a cake-tin with a removable bottom is essential, as they are very delicate when warm. If you can get a tin with a spring side as well, it is an ideal piece of equipment—for these and many other cakes.

Almonds, hazelnuts and walnuts are the most popular nuts for cake-making, and though they are expensive they do add a touch of real luxury.

First, here are two of the simpler kind—a walnut cake and a hazelnut cake. They can both be dressed up with chocolate or coffee fillings and icings, or with some of the more luscious creams given for other cakes in this chapter.

WALNUT CAKE

INGREDIENTS
4oz/110g butter
9oz/250g sugar
10oz/275g flour
2oz/50g walnuts
4 eggs
about ¼ pint/150ml milk
vanilla pod or essence
1 teaspoonful baking-powder

METHOD
If you are using a vanilla pod, scald the milk with a piece of pod in it and leave it to cool with the pod still in it.

Cream the butter and the sugar together. Beat the eggs and add them to the creamed mixture alternately with the sifted flour. Beat thoroughly. Chop the walnuts and mix them in. Then add the milk after removing the vanilla pod (or add ½ teaspoon vanilla essence if you have no pod). Finally add the baking-powder.

Put the mixture into a greased and lined tin and bake in a moderate oven, 350°F, Gas mark 4, for 1½ hours.

HAZELNUT CAKE

INGREDIENTS
3oz/75g butter
8oz/225g caster sugar
4oz/110g hazelnuts
2 eggs
rind and juice of one lemon
8oz/225g flour
2 teaspoonfuls baking-powder
1 teacupful milk

Put the hazelnuts on a tin in a hot oven until the skins start coming off and the nuts are slightly browned. Rub them in a tea cloth to get the skins off, and then crush them or mince them coarsely.

Sieve the flour two or three times with the baking-powder.

Cream the butter and sugar together, beat in the eggs thoroughly, and then add the prepared nuts. Beat again and then stir in the flour and the grated lemon rind. Add the milk and beat again. Lastly, add the lemon juice.

Bake in a greased and lined tin for 45 to 50 minutes in a moderate oven, 350°F, Gas mark 4.

SEMOLINA ALMOND CAKE

I am putting this under nut cakes because the pre-dominating flavour is almond. It's simple to make and rather unusual in texture.

INGREDIENTS
3½oz/90g icing sugar
3 eggs
1oz/25g ground almonds
juice and grated rind of ½ lemon
2oz/50g semolina

METHOD

Separate the egg yolks from the whites. Add the lemon juice and the grated rind to the yolks and whisk with the sugar until thick and creamy. Beat the egg whites until stiff and then fold them into the yolk-sugar mixture alternately with the semolina and ground almonds. Bake in a buttered and floured tin in a moderate oven, 360°F, Gas mark 4½.

When the cake is cool, warm some apricot jam and put it through a sieve over the cake. Then cover it with thin lemon icing.

AUSTRIAN NUSSTORTE

This is a really luxurious cake and makes a very good dessert.

INGREDIENTS

3 eggs
2½ oz/65g sugar
2½ oz/65g ground walnuts
1oz/25g fine breadcrumbs
a little rum

METHOD

The breadcrumbs should be rubbed through a sieve so that they are really fine. Then put a teaspoonful of rum on them and stir them round with a fork so that the rum is evenly distributed.

Separate the egg yolks from the whites.

Whisk the yolks with the sugar until thick and creamy.

Beat the whites until stiff and fold them into the yolk-sugar mixture alternately with the breadcrumbs and the ground nuts.

Bake in a well-buttered and floured tin, with a removable bottom, in a moderate oven, 360°F, Gas mark 4½, for about 40 minutes.

When the cake is cool cut it twice and fill it with the following cream:

Put ¼ pint (150ml) cream, 3 oz (75g) sugar and 2 oz (50g) ground walnuts in a saucepan and cook gently until thick. Pour into a bowl and stir until quite cool. Then beat in 3 egg yolks and a dash of rum. Whisk well.

Fill the cake with this cream and then cover it with hot, sieved jam and finally with thin lemon icing.

NUT COFFEE CAKE

A tin with a removable bottom is essential for this cake—unless you make small rounds of the pastry and sandwich two together with the cream, making small individual cakes. The cooked pastry keeps quite well in a tin and can be made in advance of when it is filled.

INGREDIENTS

5oz/150g hazelnuts or a mixture of hazelnuts and almonds
5oz/150g icing sugar
3 egg whites

METHOD

Blanch the hazelnuts by putting them in a hot oven for a few minutes and then rubbing them in a tea-towel to get the skins off. Blanch the almonds by pouring boiling water over them and then removing the skins.

Toast the blanched nuts lightly in the oven and then grind them finely.

Whisk the egg whites until stiff and then whisk in half the sugar. Fold in the remaining sugar and then the ground nuts.

Bake in two separate tins—or if you only have one tin available divide the mixture in two and cook first one half and then the other—in a fairly hot oven, 375°F, Gas mark 5, for 15 to 20 minutes—until a thin skewer comes out clean.

Handle the cooked pastry very carefully.

If you make small cakes, spread the mixture in rounds on a baking-sheet making them as nearly the same size as possible.

Sandwich them together with a coffee butter icing made as follows:

Put 3 egg yolks, 4oz (110g) icing sugar and 4 tablespoonfuls of strong black coffee in a bowl over steam and whisk until thick. Stir while cooling. Cream 4oz (110g) butter and gradually add the cold coffee cream.

CONTINENTAL HAZELNUT CAKE

INGREDIENTS
2½ oz/65g icing sugar
4 eggs
2½ oz/65g hazelnuts
1½ oz/40g breadcrumbs

METHOD

Put the hazelnuts in a hot oven for a few minutes then rub them in a tea-towel to remove the skins. Return them to the oven for a few minutes until lightly roasted. Then grind them.

Separate the egg yolks from the whites of 3 of the eggs. Whisk the yolks and the whole egg with the sugar until very thick. Beat the egg whites stiff and fold them into the yolk mixture alternately with the ground nuts and the finely sifted breadcrumbs. Bake in a well-greased and floured tin for about 40 minutes in a moderate oven, 350°F, Gas mark 4.

When cold cut once or twice and fill with the following cream:

Grind 1oz (25g) blanched and roasted hazelnuts. Put them with a scant ½ pint (300ml) milk, 2oz (50g) sugar, one egg and ½ oz (15g) flour in the top of a double boiler or in a bowl over steam. Cook them until thick, stirring all the time and not allowing the mixture to get too hot. Remove from heat and stir until cold. Cream 1½ oz (40g) butter and add the cooked mixture to it.

CAKES MADE WITH FRESH FRUIT

Plain sponges can be filled with soft fruit and cream and make delicious desserts. Cakes can also be made with the fruit cooked with them or in them or flavoured with the rind of citrus fruits. Here are two recipes for orange cakes.

ORANGE CAKE

INGREDIENTS
4oz/110g flour
4oz/110g butter
4oz/110g sugar
½ teaspoon baking-powder
2 eggs
grated rind of 1 orange

Cream the butter and the sugar and the grated orange rind. Sieve the flour and the baking-powder together. Separate the yolks and the whites of the eggs. Beat the yolks, one at a time, into the creamed butter mixture. Whip the whites stiff and fold them gradually into the mixture alternately with the flour.

Put the mixture into two greased sandwich-tins and bake in a moderate oven, 350°F, Gas mark 4, for about 15 minutes.

Sandwich together with the following filling:

Put 3oz/75g cake crumbs
1oz/25g butter
grated rind and juice of 1 orange
3oz/75g sugar

in a saucepan. Heat gently for 5 minutes stirring all the time. Allow to cool a little and then add the yolk of one egg. Stir again over low heat until the filling thickens somewhat.

VIENNESE ORANGE CAKE

INGREDIENTS
8oz/225g icing sugar
4 egg yolks and 1 whole egg
8oz/225g blanched and ground
almonds—or other nuts
juice and grated rind of 1 orange
a handful of breadcrumbs

METHOD

Butter a tin with a removable bottom and line with greased paper.

Beat the egg yolks and the whole egg with the sugar until they are very thick and creamy. Add the orange juice and grated rind and beat again thoroughly. Fold in the ground nuts and the breadcrumbs and put into the prepared tin. Bake in a moderate oven, 350°F, Gas mark 4, for 45 minutes.

Remove very carefully and allow to cool before trying to take off the paper.

Warm some orange marmalade and sieve it on to the cake and spread evenly. Then cover the cake with thin orange icing.

RUSSIAN RHUBARB CAKE

This is an unusual cake, good for people who like the taste of rhubarb but usually find it too sour.

INGREDIENTS
4 large eggs
10oz/275g butter
12oz/350g sugar
12oz/350g flour
1 dessertspoon lemon juice
½ teaspoon cinnamon
2 teacups diced rhubarb
pinch of grated nutmeg

METHOD
Melt the butter without getting it very hot. Then mix all the ingredients except the rhubarb and beat vigorously. Spread the mixture over a well-greased Swiss roll tin and cover with the diced rhubarb. Sprinkle generously with sugar and bake for 45 minutes in a fairly hot oven, 400°F, Gas mark 6—lowering the heat slightly if the cake looks like getting too brown. Cut into slices and remove them carefully with a spatula to cool on a cake-rack.

Upside down cakes are American in origin and can be made with all kinds of fruit and nuts. Soft fruits are not suitable but stone fruits, pineapple tinned or fresh, or apples or any combination of these fruits make delicious toppings. Here is a basic recipe for:

APPLE UPSIDE DOWN CAKE

INGREDIENTS
10oz/275g flour
1½ teaspoons baking-powder
4oz/110g granulated sugar
pinch salt
7oz/200g butter
1 heaped tablespoon brown sugar
1 egg
4 fl oz/125ml milk
vanilla pod or essence
apples

METHOD
Put 3oz/75g butter and the brown sugar into a largish deep cake-tin and melt them together in the tin. Peel, core and skin enough apples to put a layer of apple slices in the bottom of the tin on top of the butter-sugar mixture.

Scald the milk with a piece of vanilla pod in it and allow to cool.

Sieve the dry ingredients together.

Melt the remaining 4oz/110g butter without letting it get too hot.

Remove the vanilla pod from the milk and mix the milk with the well-beaten egg. (Add ½ teaspoon vanilla essence if you are not using a pod.)

Add the dry ingredients to the milk and egg and then the melted butter. Beat well and pour the mixture over the apple slices in the cake-tin.

Bake in a moderate oven, 350°F, Gas mark 4, for about 50 minutes.

Run a knife round the side of the tin to loosen the cake and turn it over on to a hot plate. Let the cake-tin remain over it for a few minutes to allow the syrup to soak in.

Upside Down Cake can be served either hot or cold and is much improved by being served with lots of cream.

APPLE SAUCE CAKE

This is another American cake with a very pleasant and refreshing taste.

INGREDIENTS

1 teacup unsweetened apple sauce
4oz/110g butter
8oz/225g sugar
1 egg
5oz/150g flour
1 teaspoon each allspice and nutmeg
pinch of ground cloves
1 teaspoon baking-powder
pinch of salt

METHOD

Sieve the dry ingredients together. Cream the butter and sugar and then beat in the egg. Stir in the apple sauce and then mix in the dry ingredients.

Bake in a well-greased large loaf-tin in a moderate oven, 350°F, Gas mark 4.

Ice with lemon icing when it is cool.

If you want a change from the usual fruit pie and want something that can also be eaten like a cake, you could try the following idea.

FRUIT SANDWICH

8oz/225g flour
6oz/175g butter
1 heaped tablespoon sugar
1 teaspoon baking-powder
1 egg
1 lemon
fruit for filling
a little thin cream

METHOD

First prepare your fruit. Stone plums or apricots, peel and slice apples or whatever fruit you're using, and poach the fruit gently in a little water without sugar. Dried fruit is very good but of course it must be well soaked first. Allow the fruit to cool.

Now prepare your pastry. Sieve the flour with the baking-powder and mix in the sugar and the grated rind of the lemon. Rub in the fat and mix to a soft dough with the lemon juice, the egg and a little thin cream (top of the milk will do very well). You can make the cake extra delicious by substituting ground almonds for some of the flour. Line a greased sandwich-tin with half the pastry. Drain the poached fruit carefully and put it on top of the pastry. If you are using apples you can add some stoned raisins and a little cinnamon or mixed spice. With other fruit a few chopped nuts would go down very well. Sprinkle some sugar over the fruit and then cover it with the rest of the pastry. Pinch the edges together so that they are well and truly joined and bake in a fairly hot oven, 400°F, Gas mark 6, about 20 minutes, until golden brown and firm to the touch. Serve with whipped cream—this makes a very pleasant dessert and can be eaten either hot or cold.

I think raspberries would make a delicious filling, but they should not be cooked first.

SPICY CAKES

Spicy cakes, like fruit cakes, are good keepers. In fact some of them must be kept for at least a week in order to be at their best. If your family likes them they can be made in the last peaceful weeks before the end of term, wrapped in aluminium foil and put in a tin to be brought out when needed for holiday meals and picnics. The first recipe I'm giving is for a simple:

GINGERBREAD

INGREDIENTS
1 breakfast-cup of black treacle
1 breakfast-cup hot water
1½ breakfast-cups flour
3oz/75g shortening, butter, margarine or lard
1 teaspoonful bicarbonate of soda

METHOD

Put the treacle, which should be warmed, and the water into a basin. Cut the fat into it and stir with a wire whisk until melted. Beat in the flour and finally the bicarbonate of soda. This should be a thick pouring batter.

Pour it into a greased tin with a buttered paper in the bottom (I usually use a large loaf-tin), and bake in a very moderate oven, 325°F, Gas mark 3, for 1 to 1½ hours, until a skewer comes out clean. Be careful it doesn't burn, and if it seems to be cooking too fast lower the heat. It is delicious eaten with butter or cream cheese.

And here is a recipe for another:

GINGERBREAD

This is a very good gingerbread, simple and quick to make, and as it has eggs and milk in it is perhaps better for children.

INGREDIENTS
12oz/350g flour
4oz/110g demerara sugar
4oz/110g butter
3oz/75g black treacle
3oz/75g golden syrup
2 eggs
¼ pint/150ml milk
1 heaped teaspoon ground ginger
1 heaped teaspoon mixed spice
1 teaspoon bicarbonate of soda

METHOD

Sieve the flour and spices together. Add the sugar. Melt the butter, treacle and syrup in the milk. Add them to the flour and sugar. Add the beaten eggs. Dissolve the bicarbonate in a very little milk and beat that in as well. Pour into a well-greased loaf-tin with a piece of buttered paper in the bottom. Bake in a moderate oven, 350°F, Gas mark 4, for 1 to 1½ hours, until well risen and a skewer comes out clean.

LEBKUCHEN

This is an American-Jewish recipe and it must be kept for a least a week before eating. If you follow that rule it is delicious and rather unusual.

INGREDIENTS
4 eggs
1 lb/450g brown sugar
14oz/400g flour
1 teaspoon baking-powder
2 teaspoons cinnamon
¼ teaspoon allspice
4 tablespoons chopped peel
4 tablespoons chopped almonds or walnuts

METHOD
Beat the eggs and sugar until thick and creamy. Sift the flour, baking-powder and spices and stir them into the egg mixture. Mix in the chopped peel and the nuts and spread about ½ inch thick on some waxed paper laid on a baking-sheet. Bake in a moderate oven, 350°F, Gas mark 4, for about 30 minutes. Make a very thin water icing and cover the cake with this while the cake is still warm. Cut into squares and store in a tin or jar with a well-fitting lid.

These quantities make a lot, but as it keeps so well, it's worth making more than you are likely to eat all at once.

HONEY CAKE

6 eggs, or 4 eggs plus ½ teacup coffee
8oz/225g sugar
¼ pint/150ml good honey
1½ teaspoons baking-powder
1 teaspoon bicarbonate of soda
3oz/75g each raisins and chopped nuts
2oz/50g butter, melted
14oz/400g flour
¼ teaspoon ground cloves
½ teaspoon each allspice and cinnamon
4 tablespoons chopped candied peel
2 tablespoons brandy

METHOD

Beat eggs and sugar until light and creamy. Stir in the honey and melted butter. If you use eggs and coffee dilute the honey with the hot coffee before mixing in. Sift all the dry ingredients together and add the nuts and the fruit. Mix all together, finally adding the brandy.

Turn into a well-greased and paper-lined pan (fairly shallow) and bake in a cool oven, 300°F, Gas mark 2, for 1 hour.

Turn the cake in the tin upside down on to a wire rack, and allow the cake to cool before removing the tin. Cut into squares before serving. Or slice it and spread with butter.

PASTRIES

Quite apart from the innumerable ways in which pastry is used there are quite a lot of different kinds. I am not including short pastry and puff pastry because recipes for these can be found in so many cookery books and experienced cooks have their own individual ideas and methods.

However, here are two tips on pastry which I have found very useful.

When I am making short pastry I start with at least double the quantities I need then and there. When I have rubbed the fat into the flour I put what I don't want immediately into the refrigerator without adding any liquid to it. Like that, it keeps for much longer than if it is made into a dough, and I can also add sugar to it if I want a sweet dough, or more butter for a richer dough, and so on. The rubbing in, which is what takes the time, can be done when I have nothing urgent to do. And then I can mix up pastry in a hurry when I need it.

The other tip is for puff pastry. Don't grease or flour your baking-sheet when you're baking puff pastry. Just sprinkle it with cold water—the pastry is not nearly so likely to be overcooked on the bottom.

Choux Pastry, from which éclairs are made, is not difficult to make, although many people seem to think it is. Here is my recipe.

INGREDIENTS
¼ pint/150ml water
4oz/110g butter
4oz/110g flour
1 teaspoon sugar
¼ teaspoon salt
4 eggs

METHOD

Put the water and the butter into a pan and bring to the boil. Add the flour, sugar and salt, and stir well over heat until the mixture is dry and leaves the sides of the pan. (About 3 minutes.) Remove from the heat and add the eggs, one by one, beating each one in until it is completely absorbed. The paste should be quite smooth.

For Chocolate Éclairs, put the Choux Pastry into a forcing bag and pipe it through a pastry tube on to a buttered and floured baking-sheet. Each éclair should be about 1 inch wide. Let them stand for about 20 minutes. Then bake for 25 to 30 minutes in a fairly hot oven, 375°F, Gas mark 5. They should then be golden brown and without moisture on the outside. If you take them out too soon they will collapse, though this isn't a major disaster because they can be blown up again with cream.

Fill each éclair by making a small hole in the bottom and piping in whipped cream with a pastry tube and forcing-bag. Then ice the tops with thin chocolate or coffee icing.

CREAM CHEESE PASTRY

An extravagant but trouble-free form of puff pastry can be made with cottage cheese. I find it particularly good for meat pies and it certainly saves a great deal of work.

Take equal quantities of butter, cottage cheese and flour. Rub the butter into the flour and then work in the cheese until the whole thing forms a soft dough. Chill well before using.

A more economical version can be made by halving the quantities of butter and cheese and substituting lard. That's to say, if you have 4oz/110g flour, you must have 2oz/50g cheese, 2oz/50g butter, 4oz/110g lard.

This keeps quite well in the refrigerator if wrapped in aluminium foil.

Then there is yeast puff pastry, or Danish pastry. Perhaps this should really come in the chapter on Yeast recipes, but I think it fits in better here. There are a lot of different yeast puff pastry recipes but I find the following one very good.

YEAST PUFF PASTRY

INGREDIENTS
5oz/150g flour
pinch of salt
scant ½ oz/15g yeast
1oz/25g melted butter
½ oz /15g sugar
1 large egg yolk
scant 4 fl oz/125ml milk
3oz/75g butter
1oz/25g flour

METHOD
Cut the 3oz (75g) butter into the ounce of flour, make into a brick

and chill.

Cream the yeast with the sugar and the lukewarm milk, add a little flour and put in a warm place until it starts to bubble.

Meanwhile, sift the flour with the salt into a mixing-bowl. Make a well in the centre. Drop the egg yolk into the well and add the bubbling yeast mixture. Then stir in the melted butter. If the mixture seems very wet you can add a little more flour, but the dough should be very soft, just firm enough to handle. Knead well until it is absolutely smooth. Sprinkle with a little flour, cover with a cloth and leave for 15 minutes.

Then roll it out on a floured board, making it a little thicker in the centre than at the sides. Put the butter brick in the centre and fold the sides of the pastry over it. Beat it well with the rolling-pin until it is thin enough to roll. Form it into a strip, and fold both ends to the middle. Shut it up like a book, cover with a cloth and leave in a cool place for half an hour. Repeat this rolling and folding, and then leave it in a cold place for at least 15 minutes.

You can leave the pastry overnight in a refrigerator and make croissants for breakfast. Roll the pastry out to about ⅛ inch/3mm thickness and then cut into squares and then into triangles. Roll up the triangles with the point outside and bring down the ends to make crescents. Put on a buttered and floured baking-sheet to rise, then brush over with beaten egg, and bake in a hot oven, 390°F Gas mark 5½, until golden brown.

With this puff pastry you can also make all sorts of delicious filled crescents and ring cakes. For Filled Crescents, make in the same way as croissants but don't cut the squares into triangles. Put a small spoonful of the filling of your choice in the centre of each square, then roll up the squares and form into crescents. Brush each one with egg and sprinkle with chopped nuts or sugar and bake in the same way as croissants.

For a Ring Cake, roll the pastry out into a rectangle, spread the filling of your choice over it and roll up like a Swiss roll. Form into a ring and join the ends carefully. Bake in a ring pan, slashing the top of the cake several times with a sharp knife.

For fillings you can use jam, or mixtures of dried fruit, ground or chopped nuts, sugar and melted butter, bound with egg white or a little milk. You can flavour the fillings with a few drops of rum or brandy. You can add a little grated chocolate. The possibilities are as far-reaching as your ingenuity and your store cupboard will take you.

The larger cakes take a little longer to cook than the croissants so lower the heat a little when they are well risen and brown. Both sorts can be decorated, when they are cooked, with thin glacé icing.

SWEET FLAN PASTRY

INGREDIENTS
8oz/225g flour
6oz/175g butter
1 unbeaten egg
2oz/50g sugar
½ teaspoon baking-powder
½ teacup cold milk

METHOD
Rub the butter into the flour. Add the egg, sugar, baking-powder and enough milk to make a rather soft dough. Leave to stand for 15 minutes before using.

Another, rather richer, Flan Pastry, can be made as follows.

INGREDIENTS
5oz/150g flour
2oz/50g sugar
5oz/150g butter
2½oz/65g ground almonds
few drops lemon juice
1 whole egg

METHOD

Sift the flour and sugar together. Rub in the butter and add the almonds, the egg and the lemon juice. Knead into a dough and chill for at least an hour before using.

With this pastry you can make a delicious Apple Flan. See the next recipe.

APPLE FLAN

Line a buttered and floured sandwich-tin with the pastry and bake 'blind' in a fairly hot oven, 375°F, Gas mark 5.

While it is baking, peel and slice three cooking-apples and put the slices in a pan. Add a sprinkling of sugar, a few raisins, a tablespoonful of ground almonds and a dessertspoonful of rum. Cook very gently for about 5 minutes. Allow to cool.

Put the cooked apples into the pastry-case and pipe some meringue mixture over the top in a trellis pattern.

(Make the meringue mixture by beating one egg white stiff. Add 1oz [25g] caster sugar and whisk again. Finally fold in another 1½oz [40g] sugar.)

Put in a very cool oven, 275°F, Gas mark 1, until the meringue has set.

Here are two more fillings for pre-baked flan cases made with either short crust or sweet pastry.

CHEESECAKE

INGREDIENTS
8oz/225g cottage cheese
3oz/75g sugar
3 eggs
⅜ pint/225ml milk
5oz/150g flour
grated rind of ½ lemon
2oz/50g raisins

METHOD
Cream the cheese with sugar. Separate the whites and the yolks of the eggs. Beat the yolks into the cheese, add the lemon rind and gradually beat in the milk. Whip the egg whites until stiff and fold them in alternately with the flour. Pour this mixture into the flan cases and sprinkle the raisins on top. Bake in a moderate oven, 325°F, Gas mark 3, until well risen and golden brown.

CHOCOLATE CHIFFON PIE

INGREDIENTS
1 dessertspoonful powdered gelatine
¾ teacup hot water
2oz/50g chocolate
6oz/175g caster sugar
3 eggs
pinch of salt
5 tablespoons double cream
piece of vanilla pod or essence

Dissolve the gelatine in the water over a very gentle heat. Put the chocolate and the vanilla pod into a basin over boiling water until the chocolate has melted.

Separate the whites and the yolks of the eggs.

Add the egg yolks and the sugar to the melted chocolate and beat in. Cook over boiling water for 2 minutes. Remove from heat and allow to cool. Remove the vanilla pod (or if no pod add ½ teaspoonful vanilla essence).

Beat the egg whites stiff with the salt, and fold into the chocolate. Whip the cream and fold that in. Turn the mixture in the flan cases and chill till it is firm.

If you like you can omit the cream altogether, or serve it separately.

Finally, here are some 'slices' which seem to me to be nearer to pastries than either biscuits or cakes.

LINZ SLICES

INGREDIENTS
9oz/250g flour
7oz/200g butter
9oz/250g sugar
1 egg yolk
juice and rind of ½ lemon

METHOD

Sieve the flour and sugar together. Rub in the butter. Add the egg yolk and lemon juice and grated lemon rind. Knead to a smooth dough. Roll out to ¼ inch/6mm thickness, making a rectangle as near as possible.

Bake on a buttered and floured baking-sheet in a warm oven, 375°F, Gas mark 5, for about 20 minutes.

Cut into slices while still warm. If you want your slices really elegant then you must trim the edges of the pastry before you start cutting.

When the slices are cold, spread half of them with sweetened whipped cream, into which you have folded grated chocolate or ground roasted hazelnuts. For the quantity of pastry given above you'll need ¼ pint/150ml cream. Put the other slices on top and dust with icing sugar.

BEE STING SLICES

INGREDIENTS
9oz/250g flour
7oz/200g butter
1½oz/40g sugar
3 tablespoons milk
3½oz/90g vanilla sugar
2oz/50g ground almonds
pinch of baking-powder

METHOD
Sieve the flour, the 1½ oz/40g sugar (not the vanilla sugar) and baking-powder together. Rub in half the butter and make into a dough with the milk. Cover with a cloth and leave.

Melt the rest of the butter over a very low heat. Stir in the ground almonds and vanilla sugar and go on stirring until the mixture is quite smooth. Take off the heat and stir until cool.

Roll out the dough ¼ inch/6mm thick, making it as rectangular as possible. Put it on a buttered and floured baking-sheet. Spread the almond mixture over it and bake for about 35 minutes in a moderate oven, 350°F, Gas mark 4. Cut into slices when cold.

METTERNICH SLICES

INGREDIENTS
1 lb/450g flour
4oz/110g butter
4 egg yolks
1 tablespoon cream
1 tablespoon rum

METHOD

Sieve the flour. Rub in the butter. Make into a dough with the egg yolks, the cream and the rum.

Roll it out very thin and trim it round the edges to make a rectangle. Put it on a buttered and floured baking-sheet. Spread it thinly with apricot jam and use the pastry trimmings to make a trellis over the jam. Brush it over with egg yolk and bake in a warm oven, 380°F, Gas mark 5 until golden brown.

Cut into slices when cold.

BISCUITS

It's a good idea to make more biscuits than you need any one time.
They keep well in a tin and are useful for snacks.

GINGER WAFERS

INGREDIENTS
6oz/175g flour
2oz/50g black treacle
2oz/50g butter
2oz/50g soft brown sugar
1 teaspoon ground ginger
½ teaspoon baking-powder

METHOD
Melt the butter, the sugar and the treacle over a low heat until well
blended, but the mixture must not get very hot. Sieve the dry
ingredients and mix them with the treacle mixture to form a stiff

paste. Roll out very thin—but do not try to roll out more than a small quantity at a time. The paste is very difficult to handle when it gets cold, and if you find it's getting too brittle, return it to the saucepan and warm very gently until it gets soft again. Cut into rounds and bake in a very moderate oven, 325°F, Gas mark 3.

CHOCOLATE BISCUITS

INGREDIENTS
8oz/225g sugar
4oz/110g butter
3oz/75g chocolate
2 eggs
10oz/275g flour
½ teaspoon salt
¾ teaspoon bicarbonate of soda
vanilla pod or 1 teaspoon vanilla essence

METHOD
Put the chocolate and the piece of vanilla pod in a bowl over hot water to melt. Cream the butter and sugar. Add the melted chocolate after allowing it to cool slightly and having removed the vanilla pod. Add the eggs (and the vanilla essence if you have no pod). Sift the dry ingredients and add to the mixture and mix until quite smooth. Chill well and then roll out about ⅛ inch/3mm thick. Cut with a knife or with biscuit-cutters and place on a greased baking-sheet and bake for 10 minutes in a warm oven, 375°F, Gas mark 4½.

This mixture is also suitable for using with a biscuit-press. But in this case, do not grease the baking-sheet and bake at a slightly lower temperature (350°F, Gas mark 4), as they will be rather thick and will take longer to cook.

RICH FLAPJACKS

There are a lot of recipes for these rolled oat biscuits. This one, which is rather extravagant, is especially good.

INGREDIENTS
6oz/175g butter
6oz/175g demerara sugar
8oz/225g rolled oats
pinch of salt

METHOD

Cream the butter. Mix the sugar, the oats and the salt together and stir them into the butter. Make sure they are well blended and then turn the mixture into a Swiss roll-tin. Smooth it down with a spatula or palette-knife. Bake in a hot oven, 425°F, Gas mark 7, for about 30 minutes. Leave in the tin until cooled a little and then mark into squares with a knife. When quite cold, cut into squares and remove from tin.

COFFEE SANDWICH BISCUITS

INGREDIENTS
3oz/75g flour
1oz/25g ground rice
3oz/75g butter
2oz/50g caster sugar
2 teaspoons instant coffee
1 teaspoon water
halved walnuts (if you like)

Sieve the flour and ground rice together. Cream the butter and sugar. Mix the coffee with the water and beat into the creamed butter and sugar. Fold in the dry ingredients and mix together. Roll out thin and cut into rounds—if you use walnuts, put half a walnut on every other biscuit.

Put them on a greased baking-sheet and bake in a moderate oven, 350°F, Gas mark 4, for about 15 minutes. Cool on a wire rack.

When they're cold put them together with the following cream:

Cream 1oz (25g), butter with 2oz (50g) icing sugar and then beat in 1 teaspoon instant coffee mixed with 1 teaspoon cream.

CHOCOLATE BROWNIES

INGREDIENTS
3oz/75g plain chocolate
3oz/75g shelled walnuts
3oz/75g butter
3oz/75g sugar
1 egg
4oz/110g flour
¼ teaspoon baking-powder
¼ teaspoon salt
piece of vanilla pod or 1 teaspoon
vanilla essence
a little milk

METHOD
Melt the chocolate with the piece of vanilla pod in a bowl over hot water.

Chop the walnuts.

Cream the butter and sugar. Add the beaten egg gradually, beating it in well. Sift the flour, salt and baking-powder together and stir into the mixture. Remove the vanilla pod from the melted chocolate which should not be too hot. Add the chocolate and the nuts (and the vanilla essence if you have no pod) to the other ingredients. If necessary add a little milk to make a soft batter.

Bake in a well-greased rectangular tin about 8 inch/20cm square in a moderate oven, 350°F, Gas mark 4, for about 25 minutes. Be careful not to overbake. Leave in the tin to cool and cut into squares while still warm.

SHORTBREAD

INGREDIENTS
6oz/175g flour
2oz/50g ground rice or fine semolina
5oz/150g butter
2oz/50g sugar
1 level teaspoon salt

You can of course use margarine instead of butter, but if you want the authentic shortbread flavour then you must use butter.

METHOD
Sieve the dry ingredients together and then work in the butter. Go on kneading until the whole thing forms a pliable dough. When quite smooth either form into one round cake about ½ inch/1.25cm thick or cut into small ones. Prick the surface with a fork. Bake in a moderate oven, 350°F, Gas mark 4, on a greased and floured baking-sheet until pale golden brown.

If you have a wooden shortbread mould, flour it well and press the dough into it. Take a sharp knife and run it over the surface of the dough so that it is quite smooth and there is none sticking to the rim of the mould. Then bang the side of the mould sharply on the table while turning the mould round so that the dough is loosened from the side. Finally turn it on to the baking-sheet, keeping one hand on the dough to prevent it from breaking. If it sticks the first time do not despair but take out all the dough, flour the mould again and repeat the process. The butter from the dough will have oiled the mould and should make it turn out all right. The dough is much less likely to break if it is warm from being kneaded, so if it seems very brittle work it some more with your hands.

VANILLA CRESCENTS

Icing sugar, flavoured with a vanilla pod, is essential for these biscuits to taste really good, though they would be quite nice coated with ordinary icing sugar.

INGREDIENTS
1oz/25g almonds
2oz/50g sugar
vanilla sugar
3oz/75g butter
4oz/110g flour

METHOD

Grind the almonds without blanching them. Sieve the flour and sugar together. Add the ground almonds. Rub the butter into the dry ingredients. Knead into a smooth paste. Take small bits of dough and roll them between your hands, then form into crescents. Bake on a greased and floured baking-sheet in a warm oven, 375°F, Gas mark 5, until dark golden brown. Roll in the vanilla sugar while still hot.

AUSTRIAN BISCUITS

INGREDIENTS
4oz/110g butter
6oz/175g flour
6oz/175g sugar
6oz/175g almonds
1oz/25g grated chocolate
1 egg or 2 egg yolks
pinch of cinnamon
pinch of nutmeg

METHOD
Grind the almonds without blanching them. Mix them and all the other dry ingredients together. Rub in the butter. Make into a dough with the egg and go on kneading until it is very smooth. Roll out to ½ inch/1.25cm thickness and cut with a biscuit-cutter. Put on a greased and floured baking-sheet and brush with egg white and sprinkle with ground almonds. Bake in a moderate oven, 375°F, Gas mark 5, until brown—about 15 minutes.

ORANGE JUMBLES

INGREDIENTS
4oz/110g caster sugar
4oz/110g almonds
3oz/75g butter
3oz/75g flour
juice of 2 oranges
grated rind of 1 orange

METHOD
Blanch the almonds and shred them. Cream the butter and sugar together with the grated orange rind. Then mix in the flour, the shredded almonds and the orange juice. Drop the mixture in

teaspoonfuls on to a greased baking-sheet leaving plenty of room for them to spread. Bake in a moderate oven, 350°F, Gas mark 4, for about 10 minutes. Allow them to cool a little before lifting with a palette-knife on to a rack to cool.

Biscuits of similar texture but with a chocolate flavour are:

CHOCOLATE FONDANT BISCUITS

INGREDIENTS
7oz/200g sugar
5oz/150g butter
5oz/150g chocolate
5oz/150g almonds
1 tablespoon flour
glacé cherries (if you like)

METHOD
Do not blanch the almonds but put them on a tin in a hot oven for a few minutes until they are lightly roasted. Then grind them.

Melt the chocolate in a bowl over hot water. Cream the butter and sugar, then add the flour, ground almonds and melted chocolate which should not be too hot.

Put teaspoonfuls of the mixture on to a greased and floured baking-sheet leaving plenty of room for them to spread. Flatten them slightly with a knife and decorate with halved glacé cherries if you like. Bake in a hot oven, 400°F, Gas mark 6, for about 10 minutes. Remove carefully with a palette-knife while still hot.

If you have been making mayonnaise or some other recipe which only requires the yolks of eggs you might like some ideas for using up the whites. Meringues are the obvious answer, but there are a lot of other recipes which are a bit more unusual. For instance, there are those delicious little wafers which go well with stewed fruit or ice-cream:

CAT'S TONGUES

INGREDIENTS
2oz/50g butter
2oz/50g caster sugar
2 egg whites
2oz/50g plain flour

METHOD
Warm the butter so that it is soft but not oily. Beat it lightly with a fork or wire whisk and gradually add the sugar, beating all the time until it is light and fluffy.

Do not whisk the egg whites but beat them very gradually into the butter and sugar, a very little at a time. Sieve the flour with a pinch of salt and fold it carefully in. You can flavour with grated lemon rind or use vanilla flavoured sugar, if you like.

Pipe the mixture through a plain ½ inch/1.25cm tube into 2 inch/5cm lengths on to a greased and floured baking-sheet. Allow room for the tongues to spread.

Bake in a hot oven, 400°F, Gas mark 6, for about 6 minutes until they are golden brown round the edges.

Or there are:

HAZELNUT MACAROONS

INGREDIENTS
2 egg whites
3oz/75g caster sugar
2oz/50g hazelnuts—after the skins have been removed

METHOD
Put a good 2oz (50g) hazelnuts into a hot oven until the nuts are slightly toasted and the skins come off easily. Put them in a tea-towel and rub off the skins. Then grind them.

Whisk the egg whites until stiff. Whisk in half the sugar and then fold in the rest of the sugar alternately with the ground hazelnuts.

Either drop teaspoonfuls of the mixture on to a greased and floured baking-sheet or pipe them into small mounds. Bake in a cool oven, 300°F, Gas mark 2, until they are just coloured—about 1 hour.

ENGLISH BISCUITS

This recipe was given to me by an Austrian friend who told me they are called Englander Backerei. I can't imagine anything less English.

INGREDIENTS
4 whites of eggs
8oz/225g icing sugar
8oz/225g almonds
1 lemon

METHOD
Blanch and chop the almonds. Beat the egg whites until stiff. Fold in the sugar, the almonds and the grated rind of the lemon. Stir in the juice of the lemon, and then put the mixture in a bowl over hot

water. Beat over steam until the mixture thickens. Drop teaspoonfuls of the mixture on to rice paper laid on a baking-sheet and dry the biscuits in a very cool oven, 275°F, Gas mark 1.

A similar mixture can be made omitting the lemon rind and juice and substituting 3oz (75g) chopped mixed peel for 3oz (75g) of the almonds, and reducing the amount of sugar to 5oz (150g)

The result is called Widow's Kisses!

YEAST CAKES

There is no special difficulty in making cakes with yeast. They are economical, and yeast will keep well if kept in a cold place and wrapped in waxed paper. The only thing they require more of than ordinary cakes is time. However, the first recipe needs less of that than most yeast recipes because it only has to rise once. It is called:

SEMOLINA YEAST CAKE

INGREDIENTS
2oz/50g semolina
8oz/225g flour
2oz/50g sugar
grated rind of 1 orange
½ oz/15g yeast
3oz/75g butter
2 eggs
2oz/50g currants
milk

and for the top 2oz/50g flour
2oz/50g sugar
2oz/50g butter
2 teaspoons cinnamon
jam

METHOD

Cream the yeast with a teaspoonful of sugar and 3 tablespoons warm milk and leave in a warm place until it bubbles.

Meanwhile, mix the semolina, the flour and the sugar together. Rub in the butter. Stir in the bubbling yeast mixture, add the eggs beaten up with 2 tablespoons milk. Finally add the grated orange rind and the currants.

Turn into a greased loaf-pan and add the top mixture as follows. First spread some jam over the top of the cake (it's easier to spread if warmed slightly). Then rub the flour, the sugar, the cinnamon and the butter together until the mixture is crumbly, and sprinkle this on top of the jam.

Leave the cake to rise in a warm place for about half an hour or until doubled in size. Bake in a fairly hot oven, 400°F, Gas mark 6, for about 40 minutes.

OVEN BAKED DOUGHNUTS

Fried doughnuts are a nuisance to cook and very hot work. These jam-filled buns are baked and not fried and are very light and delicious.

INGREDIENTS
1lb/450g flour
2 eggs
2oz/50g sugar
pinch of salt
4oz/110g butter
½ oz/15g yeast

about ⅜ pint/225ml milk
grated rind of 1 lemon
jam
melted butter for brushing over the buns

METHOD

Melt the butter but do not allow it to get hot. Cream the yeast with a teaspoon of sugar and a little flour (about a teaspoonful). Warm the milk a little and add half a teacupful to the creamed yeast—then leave it in a warm place until it bubbles.

Sift the flour and salt together and make a well in the centre. Into this pour the eggs which have been whisked together with the sugar, the rest of the milk and the melted butter. Then add the lemon rind and the yeast mixture.

Beat everything with a wooden spoon until it leaves the side of the bowl. Add a little flour if the mixture seems to be too wet, but be careful not to add too much. The mixture should be just firm enough to handle.

Dust the top of the dough with a little flour and cover with a cloth. Leave to rise for 1 hour.

Butter and flour a Swiss roll tin.

Roll out the dough on a floured board to about ¼ inch/6mm thickness. As the dough is very soft you may find it easier to pat it and pull it to the required thickness. Then cut into 2½ inch/6.25cm squares. Dab some jam into the centre of each square and fold the corners together. Pinch them firmly so that the jam is sealed inside.

Have some melted butter in a saucer and taking each bun in turn, put it lightly into the butter and brush some butter all over the bun. As each bun is buttered put it into the Swiss roll tin with the pinched-together corners underneath. The buns should touch each other when in the tin. When they are all in, brush them all over with a little more butter, then cover with a cloth and leave them to rise in a warm place for 30 minutes.

Bake in a warm oven, 375°F, Gas mark 5, until golden brown—about 20 minutes. Turn on to a rack to cool. They will be joined together but when cold they can be separated and should then be sprinkled with icing sugar.

There are, of course, hundreds of ways of making sweet yeast doughs, which can then be used to make buns and cakes. The following recipe is very good and the result is perhaps more like cake in texture than some.

SOUR CREAM DOUGH

INGREDIENTS
6oz/175g butter
6oz/175g sugar
3 eggs
1 teacup sour cream
1lb 6oz/620g flour (about)
grated rind of 1 lemon
1oz/25g yeast
a little warm milk
1 teaspoonful salt

METHOD
Dissolve the yeast in 2 tablespoonfuls of warm milk. Cream the butter and the sugar, then add the beaten eggs, the sour cream, the lemon rind and the yeast mixture. Mix this all well together as you add the different ingredients, and then add the flour sifted with the salt. Knead the mixture really well.

If you haven't got a wide bowl, then put the dough on a floured board or table-top so that you can turn it over and over and pummel it with your hands. Go on kneading until the dough is absolutely smooth and the surface is satiny.

Put the dough back in the bowl, dust it with flour, cover the bowl with a damp cloth and leave overnight in a warm room. In the morning you can use the dough for different buns and cakes.

For small buns, pinch off pieces of dough. Flatten them to about ½ inch/1.25cm thickness, then put some sweet filling on each bun, pull up the corners and pinch them together. Put them, join side down, on a baking-sheet. Slash the tops with a sharp-pointed knife so that the filling shows through. Brush them with egg yolk and leave them to rise until they are light and puffy. Bake for 10 to 15 minutes in a warm oven, 375°F, Gas mark 5.

Or, you can roll out a large piece of the dough—about half the given quantity—and spread some filling over the surface, and roll up like a Swiss roll. Either join the ends of the roll together to make a ring, or curve into a horse-shoe shape. Slash the top several times, brush over with egg yolk and prove in the same way as the buns. Bake in the same oven heat for 10 minutes, then lower the heat a little and bake for another 20 minutes or so.

Here are some suggestions for fillings which can be used in the same way with other sweet doughs.

Mix equal quantities of cake crumbs and ground nuts, moisten with rum or brandy. Spread over the dough then sprinkle with sugar and cinnamon. Finally drizzle melted butter over the whole surface.

To this sort of mixture you can add a little grated chocolate, dried fruits of all kinds, warmed honey instead of the sugar, grated lemon or orange rind, ground poppy seeds—anything you think might be nice.

If you are making fillings for small buns then they must of course be fully mixed before filling the buns—otherwise you'll get into difficulties sprinkling sugar and melted butter, etc.

Or, you could use your dough to make a FRESH FRUIT YEAST CAKE.

Roll out the dough into a neat rectangle and put on to a buttered and floured baking-sheet. Cover the surface of the dough with slices of apples, plums cut in half (stoned and with cut surface uppermost on the dough), or stoned cherries. Leave to rise covered with a cloth until the edge of the dough feels springy.

Meanwhile, rub together 1oz (25g) butter, 2½ oz (65g) flour,

1oz (25g) sugar and 1oz (25g) ground almonds until they are crumbly. Add a few drops of milk, or a little egg white, and spread this mixture over the fruit—it should be quite thickly spread.

Bake in a warm oven, 390°F, Gas mark 5½, for about half an hour, lowering the heat a little when the cake begins to brown round the edges. Allow to cool a little after baking and then sprinkle thickly with icing sugar.

Cut into slices before serving.

A MISCELLANY

In this chapter I have put the cakes which didn't seem to fit into any of the other categories or which I hadn't made until after the other chapters had been typed.

The first is a luxury party cake which is not baked but chilled in the refrigerator. It sounds very extravagant but it is very rich and only the very greedy would eat a lot of it!

RUM AND COFFEE CAKE

This is best made in a cake-tin with a removable bottom, but it can be made on a flat dish—in which case it cannot be weighted while it chills and will therefore be more difficult to cut.

INGREDIENTS
3 dozen sponge finger biscuits (approx.)
3oz/75g hazelnuts or almonds or a mixture of both
4 fl oz/125ml hot milk
3oz/75g butter

3oz/75g icing sugar
2 egg yolks
a little rum
about ½ pint/300ml strong black coffee (or coffee and milk)

METHOD

Blanch the almonds, if used. Toast the nuts in a hot oven and grind them. With hazelnuts the skins should be rubbed off in a tea-towel before grinding. Pour the hot milk over the ground nuts and leave to cool.

Cream the butter with the icing sugar and then gradually beat in the egg yolks. Add the nut and milk mixture and mix lightly but well. Butter a cake-tin. Put the black coffee (cold), or the coffee and milk, into a soup plate and add rum to taste—about a teaspoonful is probably enough for most people. Now dip the finger biscuits one at a time into the coffee so that the outside is soft but they are still crisp inside. Line the bottom of the cake-tin with these. You cannot hope to cover the bottom completely but by breaking the biscuits into thirds you can put a ring round the outside and then fill in the centre with whole biscuits and smaller pieces. Cover them with a layer of the nut cream, then put down another layer of dipped biscuits, then another layer of the cream and finish with a final layer of biscuits.

Butter the bottom of a plate, which will fit inside the tin, put it butter-side down on top of the cake and weigh it down. Chill overnight, if possible, and certainly for several hours.

Push the cake out very carefully, and then cut some sponge fingers the same height as the cake, and stick them round the outside. You can tie them on with a ribbon.

Cover the top of the cake with whipped cream.

You can omit the sponge fingers round the outside and the whipped cream—and the ribbon!

If you make the cake on a dish do not attempt to weight it. But it must be thoroughly chilled. It'll taste just as good as the one from the cake-tin, but it will be more messy to cut.

MOZART CAKE

This is rather like an extraordinarily good shortbread with chocolate icing on top.

INGREDIENTS
8oz/225g butter
8oz/225g sugar
8oz/225g nuts
1 whole egg and 1 yolk
grated rind of 1 lemon
4oz/110g flour
a good pinch each of nutmeg, cinnamon and ground cloves

METHOD
Grind the nuts which should not be blanched.

Sift the flour with the spices.

Cream the butter with the sugar and the grated lemon rind. Beat the egg and the yolk together and beat them into the creamed mixture. Then fold in the flour and the ground nuts.

Butter and flour a cake-tin (with a removable bottom if possible) and put in the mixture and bake in a moderate oven, 350°F, Gas mark 4. When cold ice with chocolate icing.

EASTER SPONGE CAKE

INGREDIENTS
4 eggs
the weight of 4 eggs in icing sugar
the weight of 3 eggs in ground almonds
the weight of 1 egg in flour

METHOD
Separate the whites and the yolks of the eggs.

Beat the yolks with the sugar until they are pale in colour and very thick.

Whip the whites quite stiff.

Sift the flour and add it to the ground almonds.

Fold the egg whites alternately with the flour and almonds into the egg yolk mixture.

Put into a buttered and floured tin and bake in a moderate oven, 350°F, Gas mark 4.

Remove from the tin and when cold cut it twice and fill with a really good chocolate butter icing.

Spread the top of the cake with slightly warmed red-currant jelly and then ice with thin chocolate icing.

Lastly, here is a lovely Austrian cake called:

MUERBE TORTE

INGREDIENTS
5oz/150g flour
5oz/150g butter
2 hard-boiled egg yolks
grated rind of ½ lemon
2oz/50g icing sugar
jam

METHOD
Sieve the egg yolks with the flour and the sugar. Cut the butter into these, grate in the lemon rind, and rub in the butter until a dough is formed. Divide it into two or three, depending on what size you want your cake to be, and make each section into a round flat cake. If you use a cake-tin as a guide it's fairly easy to make them the same size.

Put the rounds on to a buttered and floured baking-sheet and bake them in a fairly hot oven, 375°F, Gas mark 5, for 15 to 20 minutes.

When they're cold sandwich them together with jam and dust the top with icing sugar.

ICINGS AND FILLINGS

I am no good at decorative icing but I never think it matters if home-made cakes are not elaborately iced. A plain icing looks much better than a bad attempt at decoration, and very often a good cake is spoiled by the excessive sweetness of the icing if too much is put on in an effort to make it look nice.

GLACÉ ICING

The simplest form of glacé icing is sieved icing sugar mixed with water. Very little water is needed but the mixture should only just coat the back of a spoon. Stand your cake on a rack and pour the icing over it. Some is bound to run off if the icing is of the right consistency, so dip a knife in hot water and run it round the sides of the cake to spread the icing as it runs down.

To make a better surface on the cake before applying glacé icing, cover the cake with slightly warmed red currant jelly, or apricot jam which has been put through a sieve.

To flavour glacé icing you can use orange or lemon juice instead of water to mix with the icing sugar. Or you can use rum, maraschino or other liqueurs, or coffee, all of them diluted with water according to taste.

To make chocolate glacé icing, melt some chocolate in a little water and when it is quite smooth mix it with sieved icing sugar. A knob of butter beaten in gives a good gloss.

It's very difficult to give exact quantities, as icing sugar varies, but I'm sure it's better to err on the side of thinness. You can put a plate under the rack on which the cake is standing so that you can scrape up the icing if too much runs down. You'll be surprised how much remains on the cake even when the icing seems much too thin.

Still, the whole art of making glacé icing can really only be learned by experience.

AMERICAN FROSTING

INGREDIENTS
1 lb/450g granulated sugar
¼ pint/150ml water
2 egg whites

METHOD
Put the sugar and the water over low heat and stir until the sugar has completely dissolved. Bring to the boil and heat until it reaches 238°F, or until a little dropped into cold water immediately makes a soft ball.

Whisk the egg whites stiff and pour the syrup slowly on to them, whisking all the time.

This icing can be flavoured with orange or lemon rind, instant coffee or liqueurs. American frosting can also be used as a filling.

FILLINGS

The simplest filling is, of course, jam; the most delicious is whipped cream, either alone or mixed with other things.

You might like to try some of the following:

a cake sandwiched together or topped with whipped cream covered by a layer of fresh fruit or tinned fruit well drained of syrup;

whipped cream into which is folded grated chocolate or nuts (which have been lightly toasted before grating);

sweetened whipped cream mixed with a dash of strong black coffee, or rum or other liqueurs.

More elaborate fillings can be made from variations of:

BUTTER ICING

Basically this is butter and sugar creamed together in the proportions of 3oz/75g butter to 4-6oz/110g-175g icing sugar.

The simplest ways of flavouring this are with vanilla, orange or lemon rind, instant coffee or a little cocoa. It should be very well beaten so that it is light and fluffy.

Chocolate butter icing is made in the same way, but after the butter and sugar have been creamed add 1oz (25g) of melted chocolate—this should be quite soft but not hot.

All these butter icings are made more delicious by adding an egg yolk, or well-beaten whole egg. It would be beaten in gradually after the butter and sugar have been creamed.

Other butter icings can be made as follows.

Chocolate Nut Icing—To chocolate butter icing add 1 egg and 1oz (25g) of toasted and grated hazelnuts or almonds.

Coffee Cream Filling—Whisk 3 egg yolks with 4 tablespoons strong black coffee and 4oz (110g) icing sugar over steam until thick. Cream 4oz (110g) butter and then beat in the coffee cream a teaspoonful at a time.

Vanilla Cream—Whisk 2 egg yolks, ½ teacup cream and a pinch of flour over steam until thick. Cream 3oz (75g) butter with 3oz (75g) vanilla sugar (or plain icing sugar and a few drops of vanilla essence). Add the egg yolk mixture gradually, beating all the time.

Finally, here is an idea to lift a plain cake into the luxury class.

PUNCH FILLING

Cut a plain sponge or madeira cake into three layers. Set the bottom and top layers on one side after spreading the cut surfaces with jam.

Cut the middle layer into cubes. Put 3oz (75g) granulated sugar, grated rind and juice of 1 orange, 5 tablespoons water, 2 tablespoonfuls rum into a saucepan. Add a few drops of maraschino—which can be omitted. Bring to the boil and pour over the cake cubes. Mix in 1 tablespoonful apricot jam and stir well.

Now sandwich the other two layers together with the Punch mixture.

You can, of course, use a bought cake for this treatment. And if you ice it with orange glacé icing you will get all the credit!

INDEX

A

American Frosting, 136
Apfelkuchen, 48
Apple Cake, 48
Apple Flan, 109
Apple Sauce Cake, 98
Apple Upside Down Cake, 97
Austrian Biscuits, 120
Austrian Nusstorte, 91

B

Basic Cakes, 69
Bath Buns, 29
Bee Sting Slices, 112
Biscuits, 114
Bishop's Bread, 77
Boodles Club Cake, 73
Bread, the simple recipe, 13
Bridge Rolls, 18
Brioche (1), 45
Brioche (2), 46
Bun Twist, how to shape a, 25
Butter Icing, 137

C

Caraway Seed Bread, 61, 62
Cat's Tongues, 122
Challah, 59
Cheesecake, 110
Chelsea Buns, 31
Chocolate Biscuits, 115
Chocolate Brownies, 117
Chocolate Cakes, 80

Chocolate Chiffon Pie, 110
Chocolate Éclairs, 105
Chocolate Fondant Biscuits, 121
Chocolate Manitou, 81
Chocolate Nut Icing, 137
Choux Pastry, 105
Christmas Cake, 76
Cinnamon Ring, 58
Coffee Cream Filling, 137
Coffee Sandwich Biscuits, 116
Coffee Twist, 57
Continental Hazelnut Cake, 93
Cornish Splits, 32
Cottage Loaf, how to shape, 24
Coulibiac, 60
Cream Cheese Pastry, 106
Croissants, 40
Currant Bread, 26
Currant Buns, 27

D

Danish Pastry, 43
Devil's Food Cake, 82
Dobos Torte, 85
Doughnuts, 38, 126
Dundee Cake, 79

E

Easter Bread, 51
Easter Sponge Cake, 133
Economy Fruit Cake, 74
English Biscuits, 123